730

D0465347

FLUTE TECHNIQUE

Flute Technique

BY

F. B. CHAPMAN

Fourth Edition

London

OXFORD UNIVERSITY PRESS

NEW YORK   TORONTO

1973

Oxford University Press, Ely House, London W.1

GLASGOW NEW YORK TORONTO MELBOURNE WELLINGTON
CAPE TOWN IBADAN NAIROBI DAR ES SALAAM LUSAKA ADDIS ABABA
DELHI BOMBAY CALCUTTA MADRAS KARACHI LAHORE DACCA
KUALA LUMPUR SINGAPORE HONG KONG TOKYO

ISBN 0 19 318609 8

© *Oxford University Press* 1958, 1973

First edition 1936
Second edition 1951
Third edition 1958
Fourth edition 1973
Second impression 1974

*Printed in Great Britain by
Fletcher & Son Ltd, Norwich and bound by
Richard Clay (The Chaucer Press) Ltd, Bungay, Suffolk*

PREFACE

While some players quickly gain a good flute technique many others do so only after years of experimentation. The surest progress results from understanding clearly:

a. what muscular actions are necessary,
b. how these are best carried out,
c. the principles on which they are based, and
d. how best to form these actions into habits.

I have attempted, therefore, in the following pages to put the acquirement of a good technique on this scientific basis. Nothing will be found about the elements of music and very little concerning the artistic aspect of flute playing. Lists of suitable material for practice are however included, and Appendix II shows the extent of music which has been written for the instrument.

My sincere acknowledgements are due to Mr. Edgar H. Hunt, F.T.C.L., L.R.A.M., who, in addition to criticizing my original manuscript, has given me the benefit of his advice on many points.

F. B. CHAPMAN

READING

PUBLISHER'S NOTE

For the Fourth Edition, various minor amendments have been made to the text, and the List of Music has been completely revised and brought up to date by Mr. Sebastian Bell, to whom grateful thanks are due.

January 1973

CONTENTS

V. PRACTICE

APPENDIX I. THE CARE OF THE FLUTE 29

APPENDIX II. LIST OF MUSIC

Note

Those parts of the text which are marked with an asterisk may be omitted by beginners.

I
BREATH CONTROL

1. *The meaning of breath control.*

Control of the breath implies (a) the ability to obtain, easily and quickly, an adequate supply of air, and (b) a good command of the amount that is given out in playing. This is the first essential of a good flute technique.

2. *The conditions for obtaining and maintaining an adequate air supply.*

If the lungs are unrestricted they can become quickly and naturally inflated of their own accord by the action of the proper breathing muscle, the diaphragm, and an adequate supply of air is rapidly obtained without any undue exertion at all. In order that the lungs may be free to expand, a good position when playing is absolutely necessary. The student should stand or sit firmly in a comfortable and upright but not rigid attitude, the chest remaining raised all the time and the shoulder-blades held rather more firmly and a little nearer together than usual. Energy is not then dissipated in raising the weight of the chest every time a good inspiration is taken and the principles of healthy (and easy) breathing can be observed. For similar reasons the elbows should be kept well away from the body and any tendency to stoop forward or to lean against the back of the chair should be resisted. The head should be held up and all unnecessary movements of any kind avoided. If the air supply is to remain adequate, it must be replenished at frequent intervals so that the lungs never become nearly exhausted of air. It will, therefore, often be found necessary when playing to make use of opportunities for taking breath whether breath is felt to be necessary at the moment or not.

3. *The action of the diaphragm in controlling the air supply.*

A good control of the amount of air given out during playing is just as important as is the taking in of an adequate supply. The latter depends on the ability of the muscles of the diaphragm to contract quickly, the former on training them to relax more or less slowly at will. In order that the student may be certain that he carries out the proper muscular actions in breathing, a short description of this important muscle, the diaphragm, and its action may be helpful. It is, more strictly, a muscular partition stretching across the middle of the body, separating the chest from the abdomen and arched upwards so that it is convex to the chest cavity. When its muscles are made to contract, they draw down this arch, thus increasing the chest capacity from below. The lungs, expanding of their own accord, then become filled with air and, although there is little outward evidence of it, a good supply of air has been quickly obtained. In order to test this muscular action the fingers should be placed in the triangle formed by the branching off of the ribs on either side; the muscular contraction will then push the fingers *out* when breath is taken *in*. By relaxing the muscles more or less slowly the amount of air given out may be controlled, the fingers moving *in* as the breath is given *out*. It will also be noticed that the ribs move upwards and outwards during inspiration, and that this action is reversed during exhalation. There is no movement of the shoulders in either case. No special breathing exercises need be carried out by the student as practice on the lines laid down in the next chapter will, in time, lead to the requisite control of the diaphragm and therefore of the air supply.

4. *The management of the air supply in flute playing.*

If the method of breathing from the base of the lungs outlined in the preceding paragraph is followed, flute playing becomes a natural and healthy exercise demanding no undue exertion or strain. The student need not think that deep breathing always implies full inspirations or that a large amount of breath is ordinarily required for playing, for this is not the case. It will be found that (*a*) no great force of breath is required to play any note moderately loudly,[1] (*b*) it is by no means always necessary to play a

[1] It is no great feat to sustain the note 'b' in the lowest register moderately loudly for more than twenty seconds.

great number of notes in one breath, and (c) too much breath may become very inconvenient. Beginners almost invariably take breath too seldom and use it too lavishly: experience sooner or later teaches the wisdom of obtaining moderate supplies more frequently and of keeping something in reserve. The bad habit of 'grunting' into the flute, common with even fairly advanced players, may be traced to the lack of a good reserve and of a steady supply of air, which results in an attempt to control the breath by the muscles of the throat. If a very long passage must be played without interruption the extra effort must be made beforehand; playing to the last gasp must not be tolerated and may usually be avoided by intelligent anticipation. The main principle underlying the correct management of the air supply in playing is to interrupt the phrasing and rhythm as little as possible, or, if it can be done without undue strain, to take breath only between the end of one phrase and the beginning of the next. In very long phrases with no break it may be necessary to make one and the best place for this will usually be found *after* the first note of a bar. In taking breath between two notes which are not separated by a rest the time required for doing so should be taken from the end of the first note and not from the beginning of the second, since the beginning of a note must not be displaced. A dotted note may, for example, occasionally afford an opportunity for making such a break, this note being curtailed a little for the purpose. Breath should not ordinarily be taken between a 'suspension' or other discord and its resolution. With practice, breath can be gained so quickly that the necessary breaks for it remain unnoticeable, provided always that (a) they are well placed from a musical point of view, and (b) the breath is not suddenly cut off at the end of a curtailed note. Although the mouth has to be opened to take breath, the lip formation must as far as possible be maintained (Chap. II). Before starting to play and during rests there is no need to snatch breath so quickly, and time may be taken to inhale slowly and, if necessary, fully.

LIP CONTROL

1. *The functions of the lips.*

The lips have (*a*) to form the air supply into a small jet (the air stream) which will not spread out unnecessarily before striking the outer edge of the mouth hole (embouchure) towards which it has to be directed, and (*b*) to alter the rapidity and direction of this air stream at will.

2. *How to make the flute sound.*

Taking the head joint of the flute alone, place the edge of the embouchure just below the middle of the lower lip so that the latter covers nearly a quarter of the hole. To begin with, the outer edge of the latter should be about level with the inner. Keeping the lips gently closed, extend them a little towards the corners as when half smiling, care being taken not to turn them inwards at all during the process. The 'smile', rather a sardonic one perhaps, should draw in the cheeks against the teeth at the sides and the muscular action will produce a firmness of the lips towards the corners. Now, on blowing across the centre of the embouchure towards its outer edge, the breath will make a small opening in the middle of the lips and, when the jet of air thus formed strikes the outer edge, the flute head will sound. To ensure that the air jet meets this edge at the angle best suited to set the air in the tube in vibration the embouchure may, if necessary, be turned inwards a little so that its outer edge is raised slightly above the level of the inner. The requisite amount of this inturn must be found by trial.

It may also be necessary to adjust the height of the flute head on the lip: if it is too far below the lip the latter will cover too much of the embouchure and it will be impossible to produce a note at all. As soon as a clear note can be sustained the student should practise tonguing it, i.e. giving the air stream a definite release by pronouncing gently a syllable such as 'too', 'ter', or 'te'. Unless joined by a slur, all notes have to be tongued (Chap. IV, para 2).

3. *The proper lip formation for a good air stream and the production of a note in the first register:*

Fundamentals:

C' D''

The student must first assemble the flute. In doing so the embouchure of the head joint should as a rule be aligned with the keys which are themselved ranged in a straight line. If the foot joint is separate, it should be so placed that the little finger of the right hand may conveniently reach its keys with the least alteration of the position of the hand.[1] The student may now attempt to obtain a note in the first register. He will find b' (third line of treble stave) a good starting-point. His initial efforts at making the head speak alone will enable him to follow the more detailed directions given below and he will need to consult a table of fingering.

(*a*) Evert the lips a little as in pouting and bring them broadly together by making the distance between the upper and lower teeth as small as possible. No muscular action such as would produce any compression (pressing together) of the lips is required for this.

(*b*) Keeping the lips thus gently closed, stretch them across the teeth as when half smiling so as to give them a moderate tension. There should be no turning inwards of the lips.

(*c*) While maintaining this formation of the lips try to depress them at the corners, thus giving them a firmness on each side of the embouchure. This firmness should be

[1] It is advisable for obvious reasons not to grasp the key mechanism at all when putting the joints together, and the junctions of the flute should be marked so that they may be readily fixed in the same position every time (Appendix I).

made to extend to the interior of the lips so that it may be felt against the teeth.

(*d*) Keeping up the head, blow across the centre of the embouchure so that the air stream forces the lips well open in the middle.

It is hardly necessary to add that extensive facial gymnastics are quite uncalled for. The student should note that the tension of the lips across the teeth should only, as a rule, be quite moderate and that he need only *try* to depress the lips at the corners. No contortion of the features is required: it is quite possible to look pleasant while playing the flute.

4. *How the rapidity of the air stream is altered to obtain a note in the second register:*

Octave harmonics:

By altering the amount of opening of the lips in the middle the rapidity of the air stream is regulated. If the amount of air given out is kept quite steady, the smaller this opening becomes the more rapid will be the air stream and consequently a note of higher pitch may be obtained. The amount of opening is lessened by pressing the lips together. This action will entail some decrease in the tension of the lips, and when the compression is sufficient the harmonic b‖ (one octave higher) may be made to sound without any change of fingering. The muscular contraction involved may be seen at the back of the lips with the aid of a mirror. The student should note that he need not blow any harder to obtain the higher note and that the lips remain everted.

5. *The production of other notes in the first two registers.*

As the length of the vibrating column of air in the flute is increased, notes of lower pitch than b may be made to sound in either of the first two registers. This lengthening is produced by closing the holes in the tube one by one by means of the keys. Each successive note will require very slight modification of the lip formation compared with that used for the preceding note. The student should note the words 'very slight'. If a note can be played at all in either octave it should not be long before that next to it can be obtained. The table of fingering should be studied and the reproduction of all the notes of the first two registers should be tried. It will be observed that for the notes d^{II} and d^{II}♯ (fourth line of the stave) the first finger of the left hand has to be raised. This assists the production of these harmonics and makes it unnecessary to use so much compression of the lips (para. 4) for them as for the others of the second register.

*6. *The production of notes in the third register (assisted harmonics above c^{III}♯). Summary.*

Each note in this register is fingered differently from the notes of the same name in the first two registers and still more compression of the lips is needed to obtain the necessary rapidity of the air stream. The student is again reminded that this rapidity is not obtained by blowing harder, but by the action of the lips. The extra compression will entail a corresponding decrease in the tension of the lips (para. 3 *b*). In general:

(A) The higher the note:
 (i) the greater the compression of the lips,
 (ii) the less their tension,
 (iii) the less the aperture,
 (iv) the greater the control of the amount of breath given out.

(B) The lower the note:
 (i) the less the compression of the lips,
 (ii) the more their tension,
 (iii) the greater the aperture,
 (iv) the greater the amount of breath given out.

In the course of time, the proper lip formation required for every note will become a matter of habit and there will be no need to think about it at all.

7. *Tone improvement and first exercises in lip control.*
Owing to the many wide variations in the natural shape

and thickness of the lips in different players the production of the best and clearest tone must necessarily be to
some extent a matter of experiment.[1] When notes in the
first register can be obtained with some certainty, the
effect on the quality of the tone of altering the following
should be studied:

- (i) the height of the flute on the lip (para. 2),
- (ii) the 'inturn' of the embouchure (para. 2),
- (iii) the eversion and tension of either lip or of both
  (para. 3 *a* and *b*),
- (iv) the firmness near their corners (para. 3 *c*),
- (v) the amount of opening in the centre and the amount
  of breath used (para. 3 *d*).

Sustained notes should be attempted and the changes
must be made separately and in combination.[2] These 'tone
exercises' should form part of the daily practice, and time
will not be saved by hurrying over them. It is a good
plan to start from the note b♭ (first register) and when
this note can be played moderately loudly and with a
satisfactory tone, to proceed downwards from it, a semi-
tone at a time and then upwards. In thus extending the
range to notes of other registers the effect of varying the
tension and compression of the lips must be studied. It
may be found advisable to leave the notes of the third and,
if necessary, the lowest ones of the first register until the
rest can be obtained without undue effort moderately
loudly, quite clearly, and with certainty. Sufficient

[1] It is important for the student to listen carefully and as frequently
as possible to the best players, and to seek the guidance of a good
teacher who will also, if necessary, ascertain any peculiarities of lips
and teeth and their effect on the projection of a good air stream.

[2] After these experiments the condensation of moisture near the embouchure will often show whether the air stream is crossing its centre.
It must always do so although the opening of the lips need not necessarily be exactly in their middle—a projecting incisor may, for instance,
make this inconvenient. Many players find the centre of the embouchure (discreetly it may be hoped) by putting out the tongue.
Until its position is known by instinct it is better to use the upper lip as
a 'feeler', the player's intention is then not likely to be misconstrued
by the uninitiated.

command of the lips should then have been acquired to make the production of these notes comparatively easy.[1]

In increasing the range of notes, the student should remember that no violent exertions are required to obtain any note, and that it is by regular practice that the appropriate muscles are developed and control of the lips is slowly, perhaps, but nevertheless surely, obtained. As soon as possible, exercises and studies involving the legato (but not rapid) playing of notes at widening intervals should be attempted with the object of training the lips to alter their formation with facility. In practising these legato leaps from one note to another the student must aim at making the lips act at exactly the same time as the fingers. When sufficient mobility of the lips and control of the breath and fingers have been acquired it will be possible to proceed quite smoothly and with ease from the lowest to the highest notes of the flute and vice versa without leaving any gap or producing any extraneous sounds between the notes. At first the student should confine himself to the legato playing of intervals in one register only. Afterwards the intervals may include notes in adjacent registers and, in due course, widening leaps from notes in the first to those in the third register and vice versa should be practised.

*8. *Intonation and further exercises in lip control.*

Assuming that the student has a good instrument and has trained his ear to listen and to detect small discrepancies in pitch, he should now compare the pitch of those notes he can obtain satisfactorily with that of the same notes sustained on another instrument of the same standard

---

[1] If very much difficulty is experienced in obtaining a good tone on the lowest notes the student must ascertain whether he is really putting into practice all that had been advised (paras. 3 and 7). In any case he must be certain that his lips remain broadly flattened, sufficiently tensed and quite firm at the corners while the breath is forcing the small aperture between them well open in the middle. The keys at the foot must, of course, completely close the holes there. Uncertainty in the production of these notes may arise from a movement of the flute on the lip due to a too vigorous use of the little finger of the right hand on these keys, or to the lack of a secure hold on the instrument (Chap. III, para. 1).

pitch.[1] Since rise in temperature causes rise in pitch, the flute must obviously be warmed beforehand to the temperature to which it is likely to be raised during playing. This is done by fingering the lowest note, placing the embouchure between the lips, and breathing through the tube for half a minute or so. The note a¹ in the first register should then be sounded moderately loudly and a comparison made. If necessary the pitch may be lowered by sliding out the head joint a little. Any tendency to tune by altering either the lip formation or the amount of breath employed is avoided if a habit is made of adjusting the slide of the instrument and then sounding this note a second time before listening to the standard a¹ again.[2] If notes are being produced correctly very little movement of the tuning slide should be necessary. (Remember that strictly speaking no flute is in tune: all require some flexibility from the player.) When he has 'tuned up' the student should play sustained notes at various intervals keeping to the same intensity of tone, and afterwards test the intonation carefully. By this time he will have discovered (*a*) that his lips have a command of the most delicate modification of musical intervals, and (*b*) how easy it is to change the pitch of a note by varying the amount of breath employed.

The next exercises are therefore designed to train the lips to accommodate themselves to all variations in the air supply and to acquire that facility of control which makes the most minute adjustment of pitch possible at will. Sustained notes should be attempted in each register as indicated in Ex. 1.

Ex. 1.

The diminuendo must be gradual and even as demonstrated to the eye by the sign > and there must be no

---

[1] The standard a¹ now in use has a frequency of 440 cycles per second.

[2] If it is necessary to play to a much lower pitch than that to which the flute is built, playing in tune will be difficult. It will be found almost impossible to play in tune if the pitch is flattened by much more than a quarter of a tone.

suspicion of wobble. The intensity is lessened by decreasing—poco a poco—the amount of breath given out (Chap. I, para. 3), and since this tends to decrease the rapidity of the air stream a fall in pitch will occur unless the following precautions are taken:

(*a*) The amount of opening of the lips must be slightly but nevertheless gradually decreased.

(*b*) The direction in which the air stream strikes the outer edge of the embouchure must be gradually raised by a slight and progressive forward movement of the lower lip in relation to the upper. In this action the lower lip may be made to rotate a little around the upper, its movement being assisted by a slight forward movement of the lower jaw. Many players ease the pressure of the flute against the lower lip and retract the upper lip slightly.[1]

In this exercise the student must aim at bringing about an exact correspondence between the action of the lips and the amount of breath. Since the test of this correspondence is constancy of pitch he should, if possible, practise while the note in question is being sustained on another instrument.

Sustained notes should next be practised as shown in Ex. 2 and the intonation carefully tested:

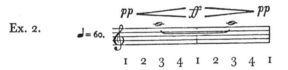

Ex. 2.

Here the fifth beat must be the loudest, viz. the crescendo and diminuendo are of equal length and the student must have sufficient breath in reserve for the diminuendo. The intensity is increased by using more breath, and since this tends to increase the rapidity of the air stream a rise in pitch has to be prevented. The conditions for

---

[1] In extending the practice of diminuendo to notes of the first register, the student must maintain that tension of the lips which is necessary to produce a proper quality of tone on the lower notes.

maintaining the pitch are the reverse of those necessary for the diminuendo:

(*a*) The amount of opening of the lips must be gradually increased.

(*b*) The direction of the air stream must be gradually lowered by giving the upper lip a slight progressive forward movement in relation to the lower. Here again the action may be assisted by a slight drawing back of the lower jaw.[1]

Notes should now be practised as shown in Ex. 3 with the object of training the lips to respond quickly to a sudden change in the air supply:

Ex. 3.

Finally, the range of all these exercises in dynamics must be extended to include the highest and lowest notes of the flute.

9. *The importance of lip exercises.*

It is necessary to emphasize the fact that the regular practice of sustained notes and of interval studies as indicated in this chapter is, in the end, the quickest and most sure means of acquiring that control of the lips on which good tone and intonation depend. Such practice, tedious though it may appear at first, becomes more interesting as the tone develops and affords an excellent aid to the acquirement of good breath control. A plan of practice will be found in Chapter V, para. 2 *a,* and the student is exhorted not to be satisfied merely with good intentions where these exercises are concerned: they are so often performed in a perfunctory manner or passed over altogether in order to acquire finger agility at an early stage. Facility

---

[1] Some writers advocate a turning in or out of the embouchure to avoid sharpening and flattening respectively. While this may be necessary in extreme cases it will be found difficult to maintain the correct adjustment of the air stream to the outer edge of the embouchure, and it is better, if possible, to make the lips alone responsible.

of finger action is discussed in the following chapter; it is, however, of little value without facility of control of the lips. Good tone and intonation must be put first and in this connexion it may be mentioned that a simple piece played with taste and with good tone and intonation is very much more desirable than a showy one performed without these attributes. More advanced students will realize that flute tone admits of endless improvement in quality and gradation. The instrument may verily be made to 'sing'.

III

FINGER CONTROL

1. The method of support of the flute and the action of the fingers.

The third essential of a good technique, finger control, depends partly on the way in which the instrument is held. The flute must be supported in such a way that (*a*) it is quite steady on the lip, and (*b*) there is little or no interference with the freedom of any of the fingers or of the thumb of the left hand. The student should stand or sit as described previously (Chap. I, para. 2), the elbows being raised and held well away (but not stiffly) from the sides. The shoulders, as directed, should be kept moderately firm, the muscular effort being sufficient to give a feeling of control over the weight of the arms and of the instrument. The latter is held against the lower lip as nearly horizontal as is convenient and the head joint should be pressed a little against this lip. This is done with the middle part of the third joint of the first finger of the left hand, the exact point of pressure being that which enables the thumb and fingers to act most comfortably and easily on the keys.[1] The top part (near the tip) of the thumb of the right hand shares in the support of the flute and should help to oppose the (moderate) pressure of the first finger of the left hand by pressing a little against the underside of the instrument. The best position of the thumb is that which gives the maximum steadiness of the flute on the lip when the notes

[1] Any excessive pressure or 'drag' of the flute on the lower lip must be avoided as this may alter the lip formation and, therefore, the tone quality. If the instrument is supported as described in this chapter this need not occur and the flute may be kept perfectly steady against the lip in all circumstances without undue pressure. If a more sloping position for the flute is preferred, the player's head must be inclined a little to the right. Many find this position less tiring for the right arm and consider it has a better appearance. Again, turning the head towards the left shoulder will allow the right arm to be brought forward a little, and this also may be found more comfortable. The beginner should not lose any opportunity of observing good players in action.

c♮ c♯ and d♯ are played in succession; it should be exactly opposite the first finger of the right hand. The wrists should be slightly depressed and the fingers, being more or less curved over the keys, should (with the exception of the first finger of the left hand) act quite freely from the knuckles nearest the hand. The curvature of the fingers will depend largely on the formation of the hand: too much bending at the joints tends to restrict their freedom and should be avoided. The fingers must, when at rest, always remain quite close to, and ready to act on the keys assigned to them: they must never be thought of as hammers used to strike the keys but as forming part of the key mechanism which has been designed to close the holes. Their action must not affect the steadiness of the flute on the lip in any way.

2. *Exercises for acquiring control of the fingers.*

The training of the fingers to depress and release all the keys equally quickly and without any excessive force or unnecessary movement is of the utmost importance. It may be carried out by the rhythmic legato practice of scale exercises (Chap. V, para. 2 *b*) in all the keys, starting with the simplest. The range should depend on the progress made in tone exercises and the speed only increased by degrees. If the scales are memorized the action of the fingers may be watched by means of a mirror and any excessive or irregular rise may be detected and immediately corrected.[1] Should some fingers be allowed to rise much higher than others, they will obviously require slightly more time to descend and, in very rapid playing, perfect regularity will be made difficult. Again, excessive raising of the fingers imperils the steadiness of the flute on the lip besides being apt to cause the keys to rattle. The slow practice of these scale exercises at first is thus essential,

[1] The mirror may displace the teacher here. Nothing becomes more trying for teacher and (it is to be hoped) pupil than reiterated remarks about this particular finger not being in a position to act readily on its key or that rising too high. Incidentally the mirror will also show if a good position is being maintained and whether unnecessary movements of the head or body are being avoided.

and a metronome should be used to ensure perfect regularity and evenness, qualities which must never be sacrificed for speed. Exercises and studies (Chap V, para 2 *c*) involving the legato playing of difficult passages should also be practised, not with the idea of rapid execution, but of disciplining the fingers to act smoothly without any stiffening or unnecessary force. Speed may easily be developed *after* this has been done. The importance of legato practice is stressed since slovenly finger action or lack of proper finger control is then shown up by the sounding of interpolated notes which have no place in the music. When the notes of the third register can be readily played, studies involving leaps (slurred and at a gradually increasing range) to and from this register will be found invaluable for training the fingers and lips to act exactly together. The synchronizing of the action of the fingers and lips is most important, and the student should bear this in mind during practice. Before these leaps are attempted rapidly, attention should have been previously concentrated on eliminating all traces of gaps and of intermediate notes. 'Festina lente.'

3. *Fingering.*

Tables of fingering can be obtained showing the different ways of producing each note. In slow passages only those fingerings should be used which give the best intonation however difficult they may be, and, generally speaking, different fingerings should not be used for notes of the same pitch that are near each other. Some special points about ordinary fingering (Boehm system) are given below:

(*a*) Any temptation to allow the D♯ (E♭) key to remain closed when (according to the table of fingering) it should be opened must be resisted from the beginning.

(*b*) F♯ (G♭) must be stopped by the third finger of the right hand unless this note is preceded or followed (in quick legato) by some note involving the use of the second but not the third finger of the right hand, in which case the second finger of this hand may be used (particularly when F♯ (G♭) is preceded or followed by E (F♭)).

(*c*) The 'double' thumb key has two plates—B♭ and

B♮ plates—which may be used to stop the notes B♭ and B♮ (or their enharmonic equivalents) respectively. When B♭ occurs most frequently, as, for example, in 'flat' keys, the thumb should as far as possible remain on the B♭ plate, and when B♮ predominates, it should rest on the other plate. When a change from one plate to the other is necessary, the change should, if possible, be prepared for when the thumb must, in any case, be taken from its key. In Ex. 1, assuming that the B♮ plate has been used for the second note of the first bar (B) and the B♭ plate is to be used for the last note (B♭) of the bar, the change should be prepared for at * and the B♭ plate used for the fourth note (d^{II}) of the bar.

Ex. 1.
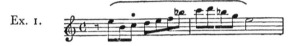

In Ex. 2 the change from the B♭ to B♮ plate is prepared for at * in order to be ready for the first note (G♭) of the second bar.

Ex. 2.

If no note occurs on which this preparation is possible it may be necessary to shift the thumb without raising it, and this movement should always be anticipated. In Ex. 3, assuming the B♭ plate is in use for the first bar, the necessary shift should be made *before* the third note (B♮) of the second bar.

Ex. 3.

This shift must be practised until it can be made without causing any movement of the flute on the lip, the best place for the thumb being such that its inner edge fits into the space between the two plates. The movement of the thumb is thus reduced to a minimum, a slight roll of the thumb engaging the B♭ plate one way and releasing it the other. When B♮ is immediately followed or preceded by B♭, alternative fingerings involving the use of the index finger of the right hand on its key or on one or other of the levers provided for the purpose must be used for one of these notes. The B♭ lever (if available) is, for instance, particularly useful when the thumb is on the B♮ plate (as at G♭ in Ex. 2) and B♭ is to be played at short notice.

*4. *Special fingerings.*[1]

Useful alternative fingerings may be found for certain notes (more especially those in the third register) when these have to be played either very loudly or very softly and clearly and in perfect tune. Special devices may also be used for the preservation of smoothness in very rapid playing, viz.:

(*a*) Fingerings which produce indifferent notes may occasionally be tolerated. Fingerings used in shakes may, for example, be applied to passages which involve the rapid alternation of adjacent notes, particularly in the third register.

(*b*) One or more fingers may often remain down throughout the whole of certain passages provided the intonation is not noticeably affected. The student may easily discover such 'simplified' fingerings for himself.

(*c*) Auxiliary or 'artistic' fingerings will also occasionally be found useful (chiefly in the third register). Here, notes below the required note (usually the twelfth below) are fingered and a harmonic made to sound by overblowing. On the modern flute these harmonics are very flat and should only be used as a last resource in very quick forte passages with precautions against any fall in pitch.

[1] Special fingering devices must not be allowed in the early stages, and only those fingerings which give the best tone and intonation should be used.

IV

TONGUE CONTROL

1. *The meaning of tongue control.*

The fourth essential of the flute player's equipment is his ability to rule his tongue in such a way that it punctuates the air stream exactly when required without in any way disturbing the formation of the lips.

2. *Single tonguing.*

The syllable 'too', 'ter', or 'te', whichever gives the best attack and interferes least with the formation of the lips, may be used to release the air stream, while the best place for the tongue to strike the palate must be found by trial. Generally speaking, the tip should not be too near the teeth, although, in tonguing the notes of the third register softly (and clearly), it may have to strike the palate rather nearer the teeth and occupy a rather more forward position than it would otherwise. The tongue has two positions only, (*a*) touching the roof of the mouth, or (*b*) hanging between the roof and the floor of the mouth. It must never rest against the front teeth nor need it act with excessive force.[1] The process of tonguing should be thought of as a continuous rather than an isolated movement. It has been aptly compared to 'dribbling' a football. The ball is the air stream and the series of kicks represents the tonguing; the player does not stop the ball before each successive kick. In the same way the air stream should be *felt* to be continuous throughout a given phrase, the movements of the tongue merely articulating it. In other words, except in staccato, the tongue is reapplied to the roof of the mouth to be drawn down again for the articulation of the next note rather than to stop the note which precedes it. The

[1] Unless emphasis is called for, the syllable used in tonguing need only be pronounced quite softly in order quickly to release the air stream. There must not, of course, be any sudden change of intensity in any note after it has been tongued unless this is indicated.

action of the tongue may be softened by using a syllable beginning with 'd' instead of 't'.

A note may be terminated more or less definitely by reapplying the tongue to the palate or by ceasing more or less suddenly to blow.

3. *Exercises for acquiring tongue control.*

Scale exercises which can be played legato with perfect regularity should now be tongued. During this practice the student should aim at (*a*) maintaining a continuous pressure of air behind the tongue, and (*b*) training the tongue and fingers to act exactly together.

*4. Multiple tonguing.

When it becomes impossible to play a long series of detached notes quickly enough in the ordinary way, or when the tongue gets tied by continuous use, recourse must be had to 'double' tonguing. Here a double syllable 'too-koo', 'ter-ker', or 'te-ke' (or 'doo-goo', &c., for a softer form) is used, the first syllable falling on the accented beat or subdivision of the beat and both syllables being of equal duration. It is better at first to practise this quite slowly and crisply on single notes. At the outset only those notes should be chosen for the purpose which can be obtained with perfect clarity and certainty, and the illustration (dribbling a football) given in para. 2 should be kept in mind during practice.

The same remarks apply to 'triple' tonguing which is used for groups of triplets. Here a group of syllables such as 'too-ke-te', is employed, the 'too' falling on the accented beat or sub-division of the beat. When sufficient control of the tongue has been acquired to make multiple tonguing on single notes possible with some rapidity[1] and perfect

[1] The student must, of course, ultimately aim at producing notes by multiple tonguing as quickly as possible: he should in any case be able to tongue them continuously and quite clearly at the rate of nine or ten to the second. If very much difficulty is experienced in extending multiple tonguing to the lowest notes, the student must make certain that his mode of articulation is not affecting the proper formation of

regularity, this tonguing should be extended to scale and interval exercises, and finally to those studies which involve rapid staccato leaps of wide range. These will be found invaluable for training the lips, fingers, and tongue to act exactly together. When this synchronization can be achieved without any mutual interference between the three functions a good flute technique will have been established.

the lips required for these notes. He should also try the effect of altering the pressure of breath behind the tongue. An innovation introduced by Richard Strauss may be noted here—'flutter tongue'. This is produced by articulating continuously or rolling 'rr' with the tongue as long as the sign ♪, Fl. (Flzng), Flatt., etc. persists. Examples may also be found in the Sonatine of Milhaud (1st movement) and the Suite (Op. 135) of Karg-Elert (1st movement). 'Flutter tongue' can also be achieved by using the soft palate, as in gargling.

V

PRACTICE

1. *The use of practice.*

By means of practice the necessary muscular actions involved in playing are converted into habits. Aimless repetition must at all costs be avoided; the mind must be fixed on the attainment of some objective and not allowed to wander. If this course is persisted in, everything will eventually become by habit quite natural and such mental concentration will no longer be required as far as technique is concerned.

2. *How and what to practise.*

Before being placed in their context difficult passages should first be isolated and played at a speed at which they can be managed accurately with good tone and intonation. The speed may then gradually be increased and the repetition of mistakes while practising, a habit so inimical to progress, is avoided. Several short practice periods daily are at first preferable to one long one because practice becomes valueless and even harmful if carried on after real physical fatigue (not mere discomfort) sets in. The habit of regular practice must, in any case, be formed and a definite scheme of procedure should be drawn up and adhered to. The time should be divided between:

(*a*) lip exercises,
(*b*) scale and other technical exercises,
(*c*) general studies,
(*d*) pieces and reading at sight.

(*a*) *Lip exercises.*
(i) Tone improvement and extension of range (Chap. II, para. 7).
(ii) Intonation exercises—testing intonation—playing sustained notes with diminuendo and crescendo without changes in pitch—pitching the playing inter-

vals, particularly fourths, fifths, and octaves (Chap. II, para 8).

The above exercises should in due course be practised concurrently, and as soon as many notes can be obtained clearly and with certainty,[1] interval and easier intonation exercises should be started. It is, however, an obvious waste of time to practise the latter exercises if they involve the production of notes which cannot be obtained satisfactorily. The student is reminded that flute tone is capable of endless improvement in quality and gradation, and that it is by the assiduous and daily practice of these lip exercises that the tone develops and the proper lip formation for each note and for every gradation of tone becomes instinctive. Students, particularly of the metal flute, are advised to read *De la sonorité, art et technique* by Moyse (Leduc).

(*b*) *Scale and other exercises.* Köhler's book *Schule der Gelaufigkeit* (Zimmermann) is recommended. The importance of practising these exercises really slowly can hardly be overestimated: the speed may afterwards be systematically increased with the aid of a metronome. The scale exercises may be 'cut' or extended to suit the student's range and the shake exercises applied in due course to notes in the third register. The more advanced student should obtain the book of Moyse—*Gammes et Arpèges* (Leduc). Here, scale and arpeggio exercises are arranged in ten different ways and a plan of practice is given which, if followed, should eventually lead to that facility of finger action which is essential to good technique.

(*c*) *Studies.* These should be selected from the appended lists so as to suit the special needs of the student and in accordance with the progress which has been made in the preceding exercises. For example, those chosen to counter-

[1] The student should be able to sustain these notes moderately loudly for five or six seconds, maintaining the intensity and pitch without any 'wobble' or vibrato. Mention may be made of a vibrato indulged in by some players for artistic purposes. This has to be controlled in its frequency and amplitude by the lips and the breath, and its good effect in solo playing is entirely in proportion to the discretion and musical taste of the player.

act any particular weakness (failure of the little finger of
the right hand or of the thumb of the left to act promptly
on their respective keys when necessary) or for the practice of leaps and of 'awkward' figures should not involve
notes which have not been obtained with certainty in tone
exercises. Again, those used for multiple tonguing should
not contain passages that cannot be played legato with perfect regularity and without interpolated notes, nor should
they be attempted at a greater speed than can be attained
by the tongue on a single reiterated note. These observa-
tions may seem self-evident, but their force is seldom fully
appreciated by students, and neglect of the principle involved frequently brings about discouragement and always
results in a waste of valuable time. It may not always be
necessary to practise the whole of a long study in order to
attain the main objects for which it has been chosen, but
the student must gradually accustom himself to the performance of such studies in their entirety; it is only by
this training that it becomes easy to keep the mind alert
and to maintain a good control of breath, lips, fingers and
tongue for any length of time. Appropriate places for
taking breath should always be marked and adhered to.
A summary of the essential objects to be attained by the
practice of studies is given below:

First stage.

(i) The maintenance of a good position.
(ii) A good quality and fullness of tone in the first register.
(iii) Equality of tone intensity between the notes of all
three registers.
(iv) The maintenance of good intonation.
(v) The proper management of the breath.
(vi) The habit of keeping the D♯ key open for all notes
except those which require it to be closed.
(vii) The smooth playing of intervals, e.g. C^{II} and C^{II}♯
(3rd space) to D^{II} above it, and from B^{I} (3rd line)
to D^{II} above it and vice versa.
(viii) Clear articulation including staccato playing.
(ix) Facility in using alternative fingerings according to
the context, especially those for F♯ (G♭) and A♯ (B♭).

(x) The development of 'weak' fingers, and of the thumb of the left hand.

(xi) Facility of the lips in playing legato leaps from notes in the first to those in the second register and vice versa.

Second stage.

(i) Facility of the lips in the legato playing of more extended leaps.

(ii) The observance of all dynamic marks without any departure from good intonation.

(iii) Equality of finger action in playing shakes and scale passages in thirds (major and minor), sixths, octaves, and other intervals in all keys.

(iv) Facility of the little finger of the right hand in the use of the keys at the foot of the flute, e.g. in proceeding from C♮ or C♮♯ to D♮♯ and vice versa.

(v) The rapid playing of passages in the third register, pianissimo and fortissimo.

(vi) The management of the breath in long passages which have to be played without noticeable breaks.

(vii) Facility in the use of special fingerings for notes of the third register in slow passages when they have either to be played very softly and clearly or very loudly and with perfect intonation.

(viii) Synchronizing the action of fingers and lips in the rapid legato playing of extended leaps from the first register to the third and vice versa.

(ix) Facility in the articulation of rapid passages in simple and in multiple tonguings (*a*) softly and lightly, (*b*) loudly.

(x) Synchronizing the action of fingers, lips, and tongue in the rapid staccato playing of extended leaps.

Selections from the following studies are recommended for attaining the above objectives:

Gariboldi: 30 Easy Progressive Studies (Augener) and Études mignonnes. Op. 131 (Leduc).

Köhler: Der Fortschritt im Flötenspiel. Op. 33 (Zimmermann). Books I and II.

Boehm: 24 Capriccios. Op. 26 (Boosey & Hawkes).
Furstenau: 26 Uebungen. Op. 107 (Leduc). Books I and II.
Kummer: Melodische Etüdien. Op. 110 (Schott).
Jeanjean: Études Modernes (Leduc).
Köhler: 30 Virtuosi Etüdien. Op. 75 (Zimmermann).
Moyse: 12 Études de grande virtuosité d'après Chopin (Leduc).

Since bad habits may be formed by practice as well as good ones it is necessary to warn the student that once formed they are notoriously difficult to break and remain obstacles to progress until they are eradicated. He should therefore continually criticize his own performance, seek the cause of faults and failures and not allow them to become habitual. He will find that they may all be traced eventually to the want of an adequate reserve of breath, or to the lack of a proper control and co-ordination of the breath, lips, fingers, and tongue.

(d) *Pieces.* A 'piece' should as a rule be chosen that is well within the capacity of the student and he should not be satisfied until it is perfect from a technical point of view. It has been truly said that no player whose technique is deficient can properly express the ideas of the composer, just as no speaker can recite convincingly if he is forced to stumble over the pronunciation of every other word. A 'piece' must never be looked upon, however, merely as a string of notes to be played, but should be scanned for phrasing and well studied away from the flute to discover the style and mood of the composer. Discussion of the artistic aspect of flute playing would be overstepping the limits the writer has set for himself, and the student will be well advised to seek the advice and personal guidance of a good teacher if he wishes to attain the end—artistic playing—to which a good technique is merely the means. Some suggestions for the choice of pieces are:

1. Simple folk-tunes.
2. Easier movements from the works of the earlier composers, especially the slow movements from the flute

sonatas of Handel and Bach. The simpler style of these writers is admirably suited to the instrument.

3. Works in the lists of pieces set for the various grades of the Associated Board examinations and for the diplomas of the Royal Schools of Music.

4. Other works.[1] Finally, students are advised to make use of every opportunity of ensemble playing and to acquaint themselves with the flute parts of important chamber and orchestral works.[2]

[1] The student is referred to Appendix II for a list of flute music. It should be noted that many of the earlier works mentioned were originally written for the recorder, although now published for the modern (transverse) flute, e.g. G. F. Handel, Sonatas 2, 4, 5, 7 in Peters edition, and J. S. Bach, Brandenburg Concertos, 2, 4, &c.

[2] Solos and difficult passages from orchestral scores may be found in W. Smith's 'Orchestral Studies for the Flute' (United Music Publishers). These contain extracts from many of the standard classical, romantic and modern works.

APPENDIX I

THE CARE OF THE FLUTE

With proper attention a flute will give daily service for many years. In order to preserve the keywork the joints of the instrument should always be taken from the case and replaced with care. They must not be held by the keys even when the flute is being put together or taken apart. Room for a good hold may be found at the ends of the joints, and a slight twist and thrust is all that is needed to fit them together. If necessary, the slides may be treated with vaseline (or other grease supplied by the makers) so that they move fairly easily in their sockets. In the case of metal joints the minimum amount of grease required for the purpose should be used. Plenty may be applied to cork; it must be well worked in and any excess then removed.

Condensation of water from the breath may be troublesome and, during rests in playing, the flute should always be held in a sloping position so that the moisture may run out without flowing into the holes or on to the pads. Water condensing here sometimes causes a pad to stick; it may be absorbed conveniently by means of cigarette paper, care being taken to keep the moisture away from the springs which, if made of steel, are easily liable to rust. A dry pad which sticks should be pressed down gently on a cigarette paper while the latter is slowly drawn out from under it. If, after a few trials, this treatment proves ineffective a stiffer piece of glazed paper which has been sparsely sprinkled with talc or well blackened by a soft lead pencil should be used instead. It may be necessary to lubricate the key mechanism as described in the next paragraph. Between prolonged periods of playing and always before replacing the flute in its case, a length of fine soft material such as silk should be passed completely through the tube once or twice by means of a thin rod in order to absorb the water which forms there. It is not necessary to dry the bore thoroughly nor need the stopper of the head joint be removed. The rod will need to be a little longer than the largest joint of the flute, and the wiper must on no account be bulky enough to require forcing; it should not be kept in contact with the flute in the case. When the stopper has to be taken out for cleaning purposes it must be well greased and replaced in exactly the same position as before. As a rule, the distance between the end of the cork nearer the mouth hole and the centre of this hole is equal to the diameter of the cork. The mouth hole should be kept clean, care being taken not to spoil the sharpness of its edge in the process.

At least twice a year those parts of the key mechanism at which friction occurs should be lubricated with a thin oil such as clock oil. It is important not to apply more oil than is necessary and to keep it away from the pads. The eye of a needle is suitable for the purpose, the point being pushed into a cork which then serves as a holder.

After playing, the keys may be wiped with chamois leather working across the flute towards the key rail; polishing the keys often results in damage to the pads and is not recommended. Dust which collects on the keywork has to be removed from time to time and should be kept away from the pads and holes in the process; a small fitch brush will be found suitable for this. Steel springs may be thinly coated with oil to prevent rusting. If one breaks or loses its elasticity it is often possible to arrange an elastic band around the keywork to act as a temporary substitute, and most players keep a few rubber bands in the flute case for such an emergency. The case should be well fitting so that the instrument does not rock when being carried and, for obvious reasons, jolting of any kind and extreme changes of temperature must be guarded against.

Every few years it is advisable to have the flute overhauled by the maker or by a really capable mechanic. 'The player should not trust his instrument to incapable hands' (Theo. Boehm).

APPENDIX II

LIST OF MUSIC[1]

ABBREVIATIONS

Breitkopf & Härtel	B. & H.
Edition Russe	E.R.
Oxford University Press	O.U.P.
Skandinavisk Musikforlag	S.M.
Stainer & Bell	S. & B.
United Music Publishers	U.M.P.
Universal Edition	U.E.
Zimmermann	Z.
Flute, oboe, clarinet, horn, bassoon	wind quint.
Orchestral version available	(O)

1. FLUTE OR FLUTES UNACCOMPANIED

SOLOS

ALWYN, W. b. 1905	Divertimento		*Boosey & Hawkes*
APOSTEL, H.E. b.1901	Sonatina	Op. 19, No. 1	*U.E.*
ARMA, P. b.1905	Sonatina		*Lemoine*
ARNOLD, M. b.1921	Fantasy		*Faber*
BACH, C.P.E. b.1714	Sonata, A mi. (Leeuwen)		*Z.*
BACH, J.S.. b.1685	Sonata, A mi.		*Peters*
BENNETT, R.R. b.1894	Sonatina		*U.E.*

[1]Most of the foreign works listed may be had from British publishing houses, e.g. Boosey & Hawkes (Artia, Ed. Russe, Furstner, Kultura), British & Continental (Breitkopf & Härtel), Chester (Nordiska, Norsk, Hansen), Hinrichsen (Peters, Forberg, Hug, Lienau), Novello (Hofmeister, Kistner & Siegel, Leuckart, Doblinger, Willi Müller, Zimmermann), Schott (Eschig, Suvini-Zerboni, Nagel), United Music Publishers (Amphion, Costallat, Durand, Elkan Vogel, Hamelle, Heugel, Jobert, Leduc, L'Oiseau Lyre, Rouart Lerolle, Senart).

BERIO, L. b.1925	Sequenza 1		*Zerboni*
BHATIA, V. b.	Flute Music		*O.U.P.*
BOZZA, E. b.1905	Image Cadenza to Mozart K 313		*Leduc* *"*
CARLO, P. b.	Filigrane		*Zerboni*
DAHL, I. b. 1912	Variations on a Swedish Folk Tune		*New Music* *(N.Y.)*
DAVID, J.N. b. 1895	Sonata	Op.31, No.1	*B. & H.*
DAVID, T.C. b.	Sonata		*"*
DEBUSSY, C.A. b, 1862	Syrinx		*Jobert*
DEMUTH b. 1898	3 Pastorales		*Leduc*
DONJON, J. b. 1839	Cadenza to Mozart K314		*"*
DU BOIS, P.M. b. 1930	Incantation et Danse		*"*
ESCHER, R. b. 1912	Sonata	Op.16	*Donemus*
FERROUD, P.O. b. 1900	Trois Pièces		*Rouart Lerolle*
FRANÇAIX, J. b. 1912	Suite pour flûte seule		*Schott*
GEISER, W. b. 1897	Sonatina		*Bärenreiter*
GERHARD, R. b. 1896	Solo Capriccio		*Mills* *"*
HAUBENSTOCK- RAMATI, R. b. 1919	Interpolation (1, 2, or 3 fls)		*U.E.*
HINDEMITH, P. b. 1895	Acht Stücke		*Schott*
HONEGGER, A. b. 1892	Danse de la Chèvre		*Senart*
HOTTETERRE (LE ROMAIN) c. 1761	Echoes		*Schott*
HUMBLE, K. b. 1927	Arcade III		*U.E.*
IBERT, J. b. 1890	Pièce		*Leduc*

JOLIVET, A.	5 Incantations		*Otto Junne*
b. 1905			*(Munich)*
KOECHLIN, C.	3 Sonatines		*Salabert*
b. 1867			
KRENEK, E.	Flute Piece in Nine Phases		*Rongwen*
b. 1900			
KUHLAU, F.D.R.	11 Solos	Opp.57,68	*Costallat*
b. 1786			
LAUBER, J.	Partita	Op.51	*S.M.*
b. 1864	Prelude and Fugue	Op.49	,,
LOCATELLI, P.	Sonata		*Hug*
b. 1695			
LOURIÉ, A.	Dithyrambes		*Schirmer*
b. 1892	The Flute of Pan		*Rongwen*
	Sunrise		,,
LUTYENS, E.	Variations	Op.38	*Mills*
b. 1906			
MADERNA, B.	Musica su due Dimensioni		*Zerboni*
b. 1920			
MAMLOK, U.	Variations		*American*
b.			*Composers Alliance*
MAKOTO, M.	Partita		*Impero-Verlag*
b.			
MATSUDAIRA, Y.	Somaksah		*Zerboni*
b. 1907			
MIGOT, G.	2 Suites		*Leduc*
b. 1891			
MIROGLIO, F.	Phases		*U.E.*
b. 1924			
MORTENSEN, F.	Sonata		*Norsk Musikforlag*
b. 1922			
PERLE, G.	Monody 1	Op. 43	*Presser*
b. 1915			
PERSICHETTI, V.	Parable		*Elkan-Vogel*
b. 1915	(fl/alt. fl)		
PETRASSI, G.	Souffle per flauto		*Zerboni*
b. 1904	(picc/fl/fl in G)		
RAPHAEL, G.	2 Sonatas	Op. 46,	*Willy Müller*
b. 1903		Nos. 7 and 8	
REINECKE, C.H.C.	Cadenzas to Mozart		*Andraud*
b. 1824	K 299		
RIEGGER, W.	Suite		*New Music*
b. 1885			*(N.Y.)*
RIVIER, J.	Oiseaux Tendres		*Salabert*
b. 1896			

SCHRÖDER, H. b. 1843	Sonata	*Leinau*
SCOTT, C. b. 1879	The Ecstatic Shepherd	*Andraud*
SIGTENHORST, M.B. VAN D. b. 1888	Rustic Miniatures	*Alsbach*
SMITH BRINDLE, R. b.	Andromeda M31	*,,*
STAINER, C. c. 1900	Cadenza to Mozart K 314	*B. & H.*
STOCKHAUSEN, K. b. 1928	Solo	*U.E.*
	Plus Minus	*,,*
	From the Seven Days	*,,*
TAFFANEL, P. b. 1884	Cadenzas to Mozart K 313, K 314	*Leduc*
TELEMANN, G. b. 1681	Twelve Fantasias	*Bärenreiter*
THOMSON, V. b. 1896	Sonata	*Elkan Vogel*
TILLMETZ, R. b. 1847	Cadenzas to Mozart K 313, K 314	*Z.*
TOMASI, H. b. 1901	Sonatina	*Leduc*
VARÈSE, E. b. 1885	Density 21.05	*New Music (N.Y.)*
WELLESZ, E. b. 1885	Suite	*Rongwen*
ZIMMERMANN, B. b. 1918	Tempus Loquendi (fl in C/fl in G/bass fl)	*Schott*

DUETS

BACH, W.F. b. 1710	Sonata		*Nagel*
	6 Duets		*B. & H.*
BEETHOVEN, L. VAN b. 1770	Allegro and Menuet (arr.)		*Z.*
BENNETT, R.R. b. 1936	Conversations		*U.E.*
BOISMORTIER, J.B. DE b. 1691	Sonata		*Bärenreiter*
CHÉDEVILLE, N. 18th cent.	2 Sonatas		*Nagel*
ESCHER, R. b. 1912	Sonata	Op.18	*Donemus*

FESCH, W. DE	3 Sonatas		*Schott*
1687			
FINGER, G.	Sonata	Op. 2, No. 6	"
b. 1660			
GENZMER, H.	Sonata		"
b. 1909			
HAYDN, F.J.	Echo (arr.)		Z.
b. 1732			
HINDEMITH, P.	Sonatina in canon	Op. 31, No. 3	*Schott*
b. 1895			
HONEGGER, A.	Petite Suite		*U.M.P.*
b. 1892			
JELINEK, H.	4 Canons	Op. 15, No. 6	*U.E.*
b. 1901	(from *Twelve-tone music*)		
KETTING, P.	Partita		*Donemus*
b. 1905			
KOECHLIN, C.	Sonata	Op. 75	*Senart*
b. 1867			
KUHLAU, F.D.R.	20 Duets	Opp. 10, 13	*Costallat*
b. 1786		39, 57, 80,	
		86, 96, 119	
KUMMER, K.	9 Duos	" 20, 69, 74	"
b. 1795			
LA BARRE, M. DE	Sonata, G ma.		*Ricordi*
b. 1674			
LOCATELLI, P.	6 Sonatas	Op. 4	"
b. 1695			
MATTHESON, J.	4 Sonatas	" 1	*Schott*
b. 1681			
MIGOT, G.	6 Petits préludes		*Leduc*
b. 1891			
MOZART, W.A.	6 Duets (arr.)		Z.
b. 1756			
NAUDOT, J.	Sonata (Fleury)		*Leduc*
b. 1762			
PETRASSI, G.	Dialogo Angelico		*Schott*
b. 1904			
PETYREK, F.	3 Dances		*U.E.*
b. 1892			
QUANTZ, J.J.	6 Duets	Op. 2	*B. & H.*
b. 1697			
RAPHAEL, G.	Suite in canon	" 47, No. 5	*Willy*
b. 1903			*Müller*
STAMITZ, C.	Duets	" 27	*Nagel*
b. 1745			

TELEMANN, G.P.	24 Sonatas		*Bärenreiter*
b. 1681	12 Fantasias		"
	6 Duets		*U.E.*
WALCKIERS, E.	Duets	Op.58	*Z.*
b. 1793			

TRIOS

BOISMORTIER, B.	Sonata (Rawski)	Op. 7, No. 5	*Boosey*
DE b. 1691			*& Hawkes*
GABRIELSKI, W.	Trio		*Andraud*
b. 1795			
GRABNER, H.	Trio		*Kistner & Siegel*
b. 1886			
HOOK, J.	Sonata, G ma.		*Boosey & Hawkes*
b. 1746			
KOECHLIN, C.	Divertissement,	Op. 90	*Editions du*
b. 1867			*Magasin Musical*
QUANTZ, J.J.	Sonata		*Schott*
b. 1697			
TCHÉRÉPNINE, A.	Trio		*Chester*
b. 1899			

QUARTETS

JONGEN, J.	2 Paraphrases		*Andraud*
b. 1873	(3 fl, alto fl)		
	Elegy		"
KÖHLER, E.	Quartet	Op.92	..
b. 1849			
KRONKE, E.	Paraphrases	" 184	*Musica Rara*
b. 1865			
KUHLAU, F.D.R.	Quartet	" 103	*Andraud*
b. 1786			
LAUBER, J.	5 Pieces		*Musica Rara*
b. 1864			
PAISIBLE, J.	Sonata		*Schott*
c. 1650			
REICHA, A.	Menuet	" 12	*Z.*
b. 1770	Sinfonico	" 12	*Cundy-Bettoney*
REYNOLDS, R.	Four Etudes		*Peters*
b. 1934	(2 fl, alto fl., picc)		
SCHMITT, F.	Quartet	" 106	*Durand*
b. 1870			

2. FLUTE OR FLUTES AND PIANOFORTE[1]

ALBINONI, T. b. 1671	Sonata in A mi.		*Nagel*
ALPAERTS, F. b. 1876	Piece		*Metropolis*
ALWYN, W. b. 1905	3 Easy Pieces		*Mills*
ANDERSEN, K.J. b. 1847	Works include: 10 Pieces	Opp. 44, 57 58, 61, 62	*Hansen*
ARNELL, R. b. 1917	Andante and Allegro	Op. 58	*Schott*
ARNOLD, M. b. 1921	Sonatina	Op. 41	*Paterson*
ARRIEU, C. b. 1903	Scherzo Sonatina		*Enoch (Paris)* *Amphion*
AUBERT, L. b. 1877	Madrigal Introduction and Allegro Nocturne		*Durand* *"* *U.M.P.*
BACH, C.P.E. b. 1714	6 Sonatas (Walther)		*Ricordi*
BACH, J.C. b. 1735	3 Sonatas (Küster)		*Nagel*
BACH, J.C.F. b. 1732	6 Sonatas (Schwedler and Wittenbecher)		*Z.*
BACH, J.S. b. 1685	6 Sonatas[2] (Soldan)		*Peters*
BACH, W.F. b. 1710	3 Trios (2 fl) Sonata, F ma.		*B. & H.* *Musica Rara*
BADINGS, H. b. 1907	Capriccio		*Donemus*
BANKS, D. b. 1923	Three Episodes		*Schott*
BANTOCK, G. b. 1868	Pagan Poem		*Jos. Williams*
BARDWELL, W. b. 1915	Sarabande		*Schott*
BARRE, M. DE LA b. 1674	Sonata Suite, G ma.		*Chester* *Ricordi*

[1] A few flute and pianoforte reductions of concerted works are included in Section 3.

[2] Also a sonata in G mi. (Nagel) possibly written for flute.

BATE, S. b. 1912	Sonatina		*Schott*
BÂTON, R. b. 1879	Passacaille (O) · Bourée	Op. 35 " 42	*Durand* "
BAX, A. b. 1883	4 Pieces		*Chappell*
BECK, J.N. b. 1930	Sonata		*University Music Press*
BEETHOVEN, L. VAN[1] b. 1770	Sérénade (after Op. 25)	Op. 41	*Peters*
BEN-HAIM, P. b. 1897	3 Songs without words		*Israeli*
BENKER	Der Abreiss-Kalender, Miniature Suite		*B. & H.*
BENNETT, R.R. b. 1894	Winter Music		*Mills*
BENSON, W.	Serenade		*Boosey & Hawkes*
BENTZON, N.V. b. 1919	Theme and Variations	Op. 17	*Hansen*
BERKELEY, L. b. 1903	Concert (O) Sonatina	" 36	*Chester* *Schott*
BERLIOZ, H. b. 1803	Trio from 'L'Enfance du Christ' (2 fl, pf or harp)		*Costallat*
BEVERSDORF, T. b. 1924	Sonata		*Southern*
BLAVET, M. b. 1700	6 Sonatas (2 fl) 6 Sonatas (Fleury)		*Ricordi* *Boosey & Hawkes*
BOISDEFFRE, C.H.R. DE b. 1838	Works include: 3 Pieces Sérénade Pastorale	Op. 31 " 59 " 90	*Hamelle* " "
BONONCINI, G.B. b. 1670	Sonata, F ma. 7 Suites (2 fl)		*U.E.* *Schott*
BOSSI, M.E. b. 1861	Improvviso		*Bongiovanni*
BOULANGER, L. b. 1893	Nocturne		*Ricordi*
BOULEZ, P. b. 1925	Sonatine		*Amphion*

[1] A sonata in B♭, edited by A. van Leeuwen and published by Zimmermann, is attributed to Beethoven.

CHAPUIS, A.P.J. b. 1858	Trois Pièces		*Durand*
CHÉDEVILLE, N. 18th cent.	Sonata		*Chester*
COOKE, A. b. 1906	Sonatina		*O.U.P.*
COOLS, E. b. 1877	Sonata Lied Sicilienne	Op. 64 " 75 " 77	*Eschig* " "
COOPER, P. b.	Sonata		*Chester*
COPLAND, A. b. 1900	Duo		*Boosey & Hawkes*
BOZZA, E. b. 1905	Aria Agrestide, Image, (etc.)		*Leduc* "
BRESGEN, C. b. 1913	Sonata		*Schott*
BREVILLE, P.O. DE b. 1861	Sonatine		*Rouart Lerolle*
BRUNNER, A. b. 1901	Sonata		*Bärenreiter*
BURIAN, E.F. b. 1904	Lost Serenades		*Artia*
BURKHARD, W. b. 1900	Canzone (2 fl) (str. O)		*Bärenreiter*
BUSONI, F. b. 1866	Divertimento (O)		*B. & H.* *(Musica Rara)*
BÜSSER, H. b. 1872	Works include: Prelude and Scherzo Sicilienne Thème Varié Petite Suite Nocturn (pf or harp)	Op. 35 " 60 " 68	 *Leduc* " " *Durand* *Lemoine*
CAMUS, P.H. b. 1796	Chanson et Badinerie		*Leduc*
CAPLET, A. b. 1878	Improvisation Petite Valse		*Durand* "
CASADESUS, R. b. 1899	Sonata Barcarolle et Scherzo Sicilienne et Burlesque	Op. 18	" *Mathot* *Leduc*
CHAILLEY, J. b. 1910	Trois Pièces		"
CHAMINADE, C. b. 1861	Concertino (O) Sérénade	Op. 107 " 142	*Enoch* *(Paris)* "

CORRETTE, M. b. 1709	Airs		*Chester*
CORTESE, L. b. 1899	Introduzione e Allegro		*Ricordi*
COUPERIN, F. B. 1668	Le Rossignol		*U.E.*
CRAS, J. b. 1879	Suite (pf or harp)		*Senart*
CROSSE, G. b. 1937	Carol		*O.U.P.*
CUI, C. A. b. 1835	Scherzetto		*Heugel*
DELMAS, M.J. b. 1885	Dances		*Andraud*
DRESDEN, S. b. 1881	Sonata (pf or harp)		*Senart*
DUBOIS, T. b. 1837	Suite		*Heugel*
DUCASSE, R. b. 1873	Petite Suite		*Durand*
DUNHILL, T. F. b. 1877	Suite	Op. 93	*Boosey & Hawkes*
DUTILLEUX, H. b. 1916	Sonatine		*Leduc*
DYSON, G. b. 1883	Suite of 4 easy pieces		*Jos. Williams*
ENESCO, G. b. 1881	Cantabile et Presto		*Enoch (Paris)*
FAURE, G. b. 1845	Fantasie Pièce (arr. Doney) Sicilienne (arr. Büsser)	Op. 79	*Hamelle* " "
FELDERHOF, J. b. 1907	Suite		*Donemus*
FERGUSON, H. b. 1908	3 Sketches		*Boosey & Hawkes*
FESCH, W. DE b. 1687	Sonata 3 Trio Sonatas (2 fl)		*U.E.* *Schott*
FINGER, G. b. 1660	3 Sonatas, G ma. F ma. D mi.		*Boosey & Hawkes*
FORTNER, W. b. 1907	Sonata		*Schott*
FLOTHIUS, M. b. 1914	Sonata da Camera Ronde Champêtre	Op. 17 " 19b	*Donemus* "
FOUDRAIN, F. b. 1880	Danse des Lutins		*Eschig*

FRANÇAIX, J. b. 1912	Divertimento	*Schott*
FREDERICK (THE GREAT) b. 1712	Works include: 25 Sonatas 3 Sätze der Sonaten (Müller) Four Pieces	*B. & H.* *Z.* *Nagel*
FRUMERIE, G. DE b. 1908	Pastorale	*Nordiska*
FUKUSHIMA, K. b. 1930	Ekagra Kadha Karuna 3 pieces from 'Chu-U'	*Zerboni* *"* *Peters*
FULTON, N. b. 1909	Scottish Suite	*Schott*
GAGNEBIN, H. b. 1886	Hiver et Printemps	*Chester*
GALLIARD, J.E. b. 1687	Sonata, C ma.	*Ricordi*
GANNE, L. b. 1862	Andante et Scherzo	*Costallat*
GALLON-NÖEL b. 1891	Suite Recueillement (pf or organ)	*Leduc* *"*
GAUBERT, P. b. 1879	3 Sonatas Sonatina Sicilienne (O) Divertissement Grec (pf or harp) Deux Equisses Romance Nocturne and Allegro Scherzando Madrigal Fantaisie	*Andraud* *"* *Heugel* *Leduc* *"* *"* *"* *Enoch (Paris)* *" "* *Mathot*
GEORGES, A. b. 1850	A la Kasbah	*Costallat*
GENZMER, H. b. 1909	Sonata No. 2	*Schott*
GERMAN, E. b. 1862	Suite	*Boosey & Hawkes*
GIANNINI, V. b. 1903	Sonata	*Franco Colombo*
GIARDINI, F. DE b. 1716	Sonatas	Op. 3 *Classici Musicali* *Italiani*

GIBBS, C.A. b.1889	Suite, A ma. (str. O)		*O.U.P.*
GILBERT, A. b. 1934	The Incredible Flute Music		*Schott*
GILLIS, D. b. 1912	North Harris		*Boosey & Hawkes*
GLANVILLE-HICKS, P. b. 1912	Sonatina		*Schott*
GLUCK, C.W. b. 1714	Ballet Music from Alcestis (2 fl strings)		*O.U.P.*
	Dance from Orfeo (str. O)		*C. Fisher*
GODARD, B. b. 1849	Suite (O) Pastorale	. Op. 116	*Durand* *Heugel*
GOEHR, A. b. 1932	Variations		*Schott*
GOLESTAN, S. `b. 1875	Sonatina		*Salabert*
GOOSSENS, E. b. 1893	3 Pictures Scherzo Fantasque		*Chester* *Leduc*
GRANOM, L. 18th cent.	Sonata		*Ricordi*
GRETCHANINOFF, A. b. 1864	2 Miniatures	Op. 145	*Leduc*
GRÈTRY, A.E.M. b. 1741	Passepied (arr. Barrère)		*S. & B.*
GRIFFES, C.T. b. 1884	Poem (O)		*Schirmer*
GROVLEZ, G. b. 1879	Légende et Divertissement Románce et Scherzo		*Eschig* *Costallat*
GYULA, D. b.	Preludio		*Editio Musica* *Budapest* *(Boosey & Hawkes)*
HAHN, R. b. 1875	Variations		*Heugel*
HALVORSEN, J. b. 1864	Piece		*Nordiska*
HAMILTON, I. b. 1922	Sonata for flautist		*Theodore Presser* *(U.E.)*
HANDEL, G.F. b. 1685	7 Sonatas 7 Sonatas (fl or vn) 3 Halle Sonatas (fl or vn) 2 Sonatas: D ma. B♭ ma.		*Peters* ,, ,, *Bärenreiter* *Boosey & Hawkes*

HANSON, H. b. 1896	Serenade (O)	Op. 35	*C. Fischer*
HARRISON, P. b. 1915	Badinage		*Chappell*
HARSÁNYI, T. b. 1898	Trois Pièces		*Chester*
HARTMANN, E. b. 1836	Sonata	Op. 1	*S.M.*
HARTY, H. b. 1879	In Ireland (O)		*Boosey & Hawkes*
HASSE, J.A. b. 1699	Sonatas:		
	D ma.		*Nagel*
	G ma.		*Hofmeister*
	Op. 3, No. 6 (2 fl)		*Doblinger*
	Sonata, D ma. (2 fl)		*Nagel*
HAUG, H. b. 1900	Concertino (O)		*Ricordi*
HAYDN, F.J. b. 1732	Sonata, No. 8, G ma.		*Boosey & Hawkes*
HENSCHEL, I.G. b. 1850	Theme and Variations	Op. 73	*Leduc*
HENZE, H.W. b. 1926	Sonatina		*Schott*
HESSENBERG, K. b. 1908	Sonata, Op. 38, No. 2		,,
HINDEMITH, P. b. 1895	Sonata		,,
	Echo (1942)		,,
HOLMES, A. b.1847	Trois Pièces		*Durand*
HÖLLER, K. b. 1907	Sonata	Op. 53	*Schott*
HOOK, J. b. 1746	2 Sonatas (Sakeld)		,,
HOPKINS, A. b. 1921	3 Pieces		,,
HOTTETERRE, J. c. 1761	Suite, D ma.		*Ricordi*
HUE, G. b. 1858	Nocturne (O)		*Leduc*
	Gigue (O)		,,
	Fantaisie (O)		*Costallat*
IBERT, J. b. 1890	Works include:		
	Sonatine		*Leduc*
	Aria		,,
	Histoires		,,

INGHELBRECHT, D.E. b. 1880	Sonatina (pf or harp) Deux Esquisses (pf or harp)		*Leduc* "
JARNACH, P. b. 1892	Sonatine	Op. 12	*Lienau*
JOLIVET, A. b. 1905	Fantaisie-Caprice Chant de Linos		*Leduc* "
JONGEN, J. b. 1873	Danse Lente (pf or harp)		*Chester*
JUON, P. b. 1872	Sonata	" 78	*Z.*
KARG-ELERT, S. b. 1879	Works include: Sonata Suite	" 121 135	*Andraud* *Z.*
KELLY, F.S. b. 1881	Sérénade (O)		*O.U.P.*
KETTING, P. b. 1905	Sonata		*Donemus*
KOECHLIN, G. b. 1867	Sonata Quatorze Pièces	" 52	*Senart* *Salabert*
KREBS, J.L. b. 1713	Sonata in C ma.		*Ricordi*
KŘIČKA, J. b. 1882	Sonatinas		*Artia*
KRONKE, E. b. 1865	Works include: Suites	Opp. 81, 164, 165, 171	*Z.*
KRUMPHOLZ, J.B. b. 1745	Sonata (pf or harp)		*Nagel*
KUBIK, G. b. 1914	Nocturne		*Schirmer*
KUHLAU, F.D.R. b. 1786	Works include: 2 Sonatas 3 Solos 2 Fantasias	" 83, 85 Op. 57 " 95	*Schmidt* *Costallat* "
LACOMBE, P. b. 1837	Conte d'Hiver		*Costallat*
LAUBER, J. b. 1864	2 Sonatas Tanz Suite Aubade 4 Danses (pf or harp)	Opp. 50, 53 Op. 48 " 45	*S.M.* " *Heugel* *Z.*
LAPIS, S. 18th cent.	3 Easy Sonatas		*Schott*
LECLAIR, J.M. b. 1697	4 Sonatas: G ma. E mi. C ma. B mi.		*Schott* *Ricordi*

LEIGH, W. b. 1905	Sonatina		*Schott*
LEROUX, X. b. 1863	2 Romances		*Leduc*
LINICKE, J.G. b. 1695	2 Suites (2 fl)		*Peters*
LOCATELLI, P. b. 1695	3 Sonatas (Scheck) 3 Sonatas (2 fl)	Op. 5, Nos. 1, 4, 5	*Bärenreiter* *Kistner & Siegel*
LOEILLET, J.B. b. 1653	6 Sonatas 2 Sonatas, E mi. G mi. (2 fl)	" 3	*Schott* *Lemoine*
LOTHAR, M. b. 1902	Sonata		*Kistner & Siegel*
LULLY, J.B. b. 1632	20 Pieces (arr. Matthes)		*Hug*
MACKLEAN, C. 18th cent.	Sonata No. 9 (arr. Bullock)		*O.U.P.*
MADERNA, B. b. 1920	Honeyrèves		*Zerboni*
MAGANINI, Q. b. 1897	Works include: Sonata Gauloise		*C. Fisher*
MARCELLO, B. b. 1686	3 Sonatas F ma. G ma. B♭ ma.		*O.U.P.*
MARTELLI, H. b. 1895	Sonata Fantasiestuck	Op. 67	*Schott* *Leduc*
MARTIN, F. b. 1890	Ballade (O)		*U.E.*
MARTINU, B. b. 1890	Sonata		*Schott*
MARX, K. b. 1897	Sonatina, G ma. (recorder)		*Bärenreiter*
MARZELLIER, J. b. 1879	Divertissement		*Costallat*
MATSUDAIRA, Y. b. 1907	Sonatine		*Shawnee Press*
MATTHESON, J. b. 1681	12 Krammer Sonatas (van Leeuwen)		*Z.*
MAW, N. b. 1935	Sonatina		*Chester*
MERCADANTI, J. b. 1795	2 Pieces		*Hinrichsen*
MESSIAEN, O. b. 1908	Le Merle Noir		*Leduc*
MIGOT, G. b. 1891	Sonata		"

MILFORD, R. b. 1903	Sonata, C ma.		*Augener*
MILHAUD, D. b. 1892	Sonatine		*Durand*
MORITZ, E. b. 1891	Kleine Sonata	Op. 49	*Z.*
MOUQUET, J. b. 1867	Works include: Flûte de Pan (O) Berceuse Eglogue Cinq pièces brèves	,, 15 ,, 22 ,, 29 ,, 39	*Lemoine* ,, ,, ,,
MOZART, W.A. b. 1756	Six Sonatas		*Reinhardt*
MULDER, H. b. 1898	Sonata		*Donemus*
MURRILL, H. b. 1909	Sonata		*O.U.P.*
NIEMANN, W. b. 1876	Vier Stücke	Op. 121a	*Z.*
NIELSEN, C. b. 1865	'The fog lifts'		*Hansen*
NORDOFF, P. b. 1909	Dance Sonata		*New Music (N.Y.)*
OLLONE, M.D. b. 1875	Nocturne Andante and Allegro		*U.M.P.* ,,
PEPUSCH, J.C. b. 1667	6 Sonatas (Giesbert)		*Schott*
PESSARD, E.L.F. b. 1843	Valse Tendre		*Lemoine*
PIJPER, W. b. 1894	Sonata		*O.U.P.*
PILLIOS, J. b. 1877	Bucoliques		*Senart*
PISTON, W. b. 1894	Sonata		*Andraud*
PITFIELD, T.B. b. 1903	Sonatina		*O.U.P.*
PLATTI, G. b. 1700	3 Sonatas (Jarnach)		*Schott*
POOT, M. b. 1901	Sicilienne		*Leduc*
POULENC b. 1899	Sonata		*Chester*
PROKOFIEF, S. b. 1891	Sonata	Op. 94	*Boosey & Hawkes*

PURCELL, D.	2 Sonatas, F ma. and		Schott
b. 1660	D mi.		
PURCELL, H.	Air and Hornpipe		Boosey & Hawkes
b. 1658	(arr. Revell)		
QUANTZ, J.J.	Works include 2 Sonatas:		
b. 1697	C ma. (2 fl)		Bärenreiter
	E mi.		B. & H.
	6 Sonatas		Musica Rara
	Arioso and Presto		Southern
RAMEAU, J.P.	Sarabande		S. & B.
b. 1683	(arr. Barrère)		
RAPHAEL, G.	Sonata, E mi.		B. & H.
b. 1903			
RAVEL, M.	Pièce (arr. Fleury)		Leduc
b. 1875			
REGER, M.	Romance in G		B. & H.
b. 1873	(Schwedler)		
REIZENSTEIN, F.	Partita		Schott
b. 1911			
RENOSTO, P.	Mixage		Ricordi
RHEINBERGER, J.	Rhapsodie		Kistner & Siegel
b. 1839			
RHENÉ-BATON	Passacaille (O)	Op. 35	Durand
b. 1879	Bourée	" 42	"
RICHARDSON, A.	Sonatina		Weinberger
b. 1904			
RICHTER, F.X.	Sonata, G ma.		Schott
b. 1709			
RIETI, V.	Sonatine		Bongiovanni
b. 1898			
RIMSKY-	Hummelflug		Boosey & Hawkes
KORSAKOV, N.A.	(arr. Strimer)		
b. 1844			
ROMAN, J.H.	4 Sonatas (Senn)		Lienau
b. 1694			
ROOTHAM, C.B.	Suite		Chester
b. 1875			
ROPARTZ, J.G.	Sonatine		Durand
b. 1864			
ROUSSEL, A.C.P.	Joueurs de Flûte	Op. 27	Durand
b. 1869	Andante and Scherzo	" 51	"
	Aria (O)		Leduc
ROWLEY, A.	Humoresque (O)		Ashdown
b. 1892	Pastoral Elegy		Jos. Williams
	Pavane and Dance		Boosey & Hawkes

ROYER, E. b. 1882	Quatre Pièces		*Senart*
RUBBRA, E. b. 1901	Meditationi Sopra 'Coeurs désolés' (recorder and harpsichord)		*Lengnick*
RUYNEMAN, D. b. 1886	Sonata 4 Songs		*Donemus* "
SAINT-SAËNS, C. b. 1835	Romance (O) Odelette (O) Volière (trans. from 'Carnival of Animals')	Op. 37 Op. 162	*Durand* " "
SAMAZEUILH, G. b. 1877	Chant sans paroles Equisse d'Espagne Luciole		" " "
SAMMARTINI 18th cent.	12 Sonatas (Giesbert) (2 fl)		*Schott*
SAUGUET, H. b. 1901	Sonatine		*Rouart Lerolle*
SCARLATTI, A. b. 1659	Quartettino (3 fl)		*Peters*
SCARLATTI, D b. 1685	Sonata, D mi. (arr. Rofe)		*Boosey & Hawkes*
	2 Sonatas, E mi. G mi. (arr. Leeuwen)		*Schirmer*
SCARLATTI-BENJAMIN b. 1683 b. 1893	Suite (str. O)		*Boosey & Hawkes*
SCHICKHARD, J.C. c. 1730	6 Sonatas Concerto (Knab) (4 fl)	Op. 1	*Schott* *Bärenreiter*
SCHMITT, FLORENT b. 1870	Suite Scherzo Pastorale	Op. 129	*U.M.P.* *International*
SCHOENBERG, A. b. 1874	Sonata (after the quintet)	Op. 26	*U.E.*
SCHOUWMAN, H. b. 1902	4 Pieces	Op. 39	*Donemus*
SCHUBERT, F. b. 1797	Introduction and Variations	Op. 160	*Hinrichsen*
SCHULHOFF, E. b. 1894	Sonata		*Chester*
SCHURMANN, G. b. 1928	Sonatina		*Fairfield (Novello)*
SCOTT, C. b. 1879	Aubade Scottish Pastoral		*Schott* *Hansen*

SEARLE, H.	Divertimento		*Schott*
b. 1915			
SEIBER, M.	Pastorale and		"
b. 1905	Burlesque (str. O)		
SHAW, M.	Sonata, E♭ ma.		*Cramer*
b. 1875			
SMIT, L.	Sonata		*Donemus*
b. 1900			
SPAIN-DUNK, S.	'The Water Lily Pool'		*Elkin*
b. 1885	(str. O)		
SPELMAN, T.M.	Rondo		*Chester*
b. 1891			
SPINKS, C.	Pebmarsh Fancy		*O.U.P.*
b. 1915			
STANLEY, J.	Sonata, A ma.		*Ricordi*
b. 1713	4 Solos	Op. 1, Nos. 1, 2, 12	*Boosey & Hawkes*
STOCKHAUSEN, K.	Plus Minus		*U.E.*
b. 1928	From the Seven Days		"
STOKER, R.	Sonatina		*Hinrichsen*
b. 1938			
SVENDSEN, J.	Romance (Barge)	Op. 26	*Hansen*
b. 1840			
SZERVANSKY, E.	Sonatina		*Kultura*
b. 1912			
TAFFANEL, P.	Andante, Pastorale and		*International*
b. 1844	Scherzettino		
TAILLEFERRE, G.	Pastorale		*Elkan-Vogel*
b. 1892			
TANSMAN, A.	Sonatine		*Senart*
b. 1897			
TARP, S.E.	Concertino	Op. 30	*Chester*
b. 1908			
TCHAIKOWSKY, P.	Dance des Mirlitons		*C. Fisher*
b. 1840	(arr. 3 fl, pf)		
TELEMANN, G.P.	Sonatas:		
b. 1681	C ma. C ma. D mi.		*Peters*
	D ma. F ma.		*Nagel*
	G ma.		*Schott*
	B mi.		*B. & H.*
	12 Methodische		*Bärenreiter*
	Sonaten		
	C ma. (2 fl)		*Bärenreiter*
	F ma. A ma. (2 fl)		*B. & H.*
	3 Scherzi (2 fl)		"

TEMPLETON, A b. 1909	Siciliana		*Leeds*
TOGNI, C. b. 1922	Sonata	Op. 35	*U.E.*
TOMASI, H. b. 1901	Concertino, E ma. (O) Le petit chevrier Corse (pf or harp)		*Leduc* *Otto Junne* *(Munich)*
TULOU, J.L. b. 1786	Works include: Fantasie	Op. 29	*Costallat*
VALENTINO, R. 18th cent.	3 Sonatas		*Nagel*
VERACINI, F.M. b. 1690	2 Sonatas		*Boosey & Hawkes*
VITTADINI, F. b. 1884	Elegy		*U.M.P.*
VIVALDI, A. b. 1680	Sonata, G mi. " C ma.		*Schott* *Chester*
VREULS, V. b. 1876	Elegie (O)		*Bosworth*
WALTHEW, R.H. b. 1872	Idyll		*S. & B.*
WANHAL, J. b. 1739	Sonatina		*Hinrichsen*
WEBER, C.M. VON b. 1786	Romanza Siciliana (O)		*Lienau*
WEHRLI, W. b. 1892	Suite	Op. 16	*Hug*
WEINBERGER, J. b. 1896	Sonatina		*C. Fisher*
WIDOR, C.M. b. 1845	Suite	Op. 34	*Heugel*
WIJDEVELD, W. b. 1910	Sonatine		*Donemus*
ZAGWIJN, H. b. 1878	Capriccio Sonata		*"* *"*
ZIPOLI, D. b. 1688	Sarabanda e Giga (Setaccioli)		*Ricordi*

3. QUINTETS, LARGER COMBINATIONS

ADDISON, J. b. 1920	Serenade wind quint, harp	*O.U.P.*
ALWYN, W. b. 1905	Concerto fl, ob, 2 horns, trpt, strings, perc	*Lengnick*

ANDRIESSEN, H. b. 1892	Variations on a Theme of Couperin fl, strings, harp		*Donemus*
ANDRIESSEN, J. b. 1925	Hommage à Milhaud fl, str quart Octet fl, 2 ob, 2 cl, bass cl, 2 fag Concerto fl, orch		,, ,, ,,
ANGERER, P. b. 1927	Octet wind quint, 2 trpt, tromb		*U.E.*
ARMA, P. b. 1904	Sept Transparences		*Lemoine*
ARNE, T.A. b. 1710	Suite of Dances (arr. Collins) wind quint		*Keith Prowse*
ARNOLD, M. b. 1921	Concerto fl, strings 3 Shanties wind quint	Op. 45	*Paterson* ,,
BACH, C.P.E. b. 1714	3 Sonatinas 2 fl, 2 vn, va, vc, clav C ma. E♭ ma., D mi. 2 Concertos, G ma. A mi fl, strings		 *Hinrichsen* *Bärenreiter* *Hinrichsen*
BACH, J.C. b. 1735	2 Quintets (Steglich) fl, ob, vn, va, vc, clav Divertissement 2 fl, orch 2 fl, pf, arr.	Op. 11, Nos 4, 6	*Nagel* *Andraud*
BACH, J.S.[1] b.1685	Overture, B mi. fl, strings, clav fl, pf, (arr. Callimahos) 3 Brandenburg Concertos No. 2, F ma. fl, ob, trpt, vn, strings		*B. & H.* *Schott* *B. & H.*

[1] Arrangements include: 'The Art of Fugue', 7 winds, strings, harpsichord (Augener) or 10 winds, strings (Peters). The '48' (No. 22), wind quintet (Hinrichsen).

BACH, J.S.	No. 4, G ma.	
b. 1685	2 fl, vn, strings	
(continued)	No. 5, D ma.	
	clav, fl, vn, strings	
	Concerto (after No. 4),	*B. & H.*
	F ma.	
	2 fl, clav, strings	
	Triple Concerto No. 2,	"
	A mi.	
	clav, fl, vn, strings	*(Musica Rara)*
BADINGS, H.	2 Quintets	*Donemus*
b. 1907	wind quint	
	Capriccio	"
	fl, vn, va, harp	
BARBER, S.	Capricorn Concerto	*Schirmer*
b. 1910	fl, ob, trpt, strings	
	Summer Music	
BAX, A.	Concerto	*Chappell*
b. 1883	fl, ob, harp, str quart	
	Nonet	
	fl, ob, cl, harp, str	"
	quint	
BECK, C.	Serenade	*Schott*
b. 1901	fl, cl, strings	
BEDFORD, D.	Pentomino	*U.E.*
b. 1937		
BEDFORD, H.	Lyric Interlude Op. 50	*Chester*
b. 1867	pf, fl, ob, vn, va	
	Oriental Dance	
	fl, trpt, perc, strings	"
BENNETT, R.R.	Quintet	*U.E.*
b. 1894		
BENTZON, J.	Racconto " 46, No. 5	*S.M.*
b. 1897	wind quint	
BEREZOVSKY, N.	Suite " 11	*E.R.*
b. 1900	fl, ob, cl, cor angl, fag	
BERIO, L.	Opus no. 700	*U.E.*
b. 1925		
BIRTWISTLE, H.	Refrains and Choruses	"
b. 1934		
BIZET, G.	Menuet from 2nd Arle-	*Otto Junne*
b. 1838	sienne Suite	*(Munich)*
	fl, orch	
BLATCHER, B.	Dialogue	*U.E.*
b. 1903	fl, vn, pf, strings	

BLISS, A.	Conversations		*Curwen*
b. 1891	fl (bass fl), ob (cor angl), vn, va, vc		
BLOCH, E.	Concertino		*Schirmer*
b. 1880	fl, va, strings		
	fl, va, pf, arr.		
BLUMER, T.	Quintet	Op. 52	*Sikorski*
b. 1882	wind quint		
	Musikalische Bilder	" 69	*Z.*
	fl, Orch		
	Concert giocoso	" 98	"
	fl, orch		
BOCCHERINI, L.	Concerto, D ma.	" 27	*Nagel*
b. 1743	fl, strings		
	Sextet	" 42, No. 2	*Sikorski*
	fl, horn, fag, vn, va, db		
BOISDEFFRE, C.H.R. DE	Scherzo from Sextet	" 49	*U.M.P.*
b. 1838	pf, wind quint, db		
BOISMORTIER, J.B. DE b. 1691	Concerto		*Ricordi*
	fl, vn, ob, fag, clav		
BORDES, C.	Suite Basque	" 6	*Bornemann*
b. 1863	fl, str quint		*(Paris)*
BORKOVEC, P.	Nonet		*Hudebni Matice*
b. 1894	wind quint, vn, va, vc, db		*(Artia)*
BOROWSKI, F.	Madrigal		*Boosey & Hawkes*
b. 1872	wind quint		
BRANDTS-BUYS, J.	Quintet	" 6	*Doblinger*
b. 1812	fl, str quart		*(Musica Rara)*
BRITTEN, B.	Sinfonietta	" 1	*Boosey & Hawkes*
b. 1913	wind quint, strings		
BURKHARD, W.	Serenade	" 77 "	"
b. 1900	fl, cl, fag, horn, vn, va, harp, db		
CARTER, E.	Quintet		*Assoc. Music Pub.*
b. 1908	wind quint		*(N.Y.)*
CASADESUS, R.M.	Dixtuor		*Andraud*
b. 1899	double wind quint		
CHAGRIN, F.	Divertimento		*Augener*
b. 1905	wind quint		
CIMAROSA, D.	Concerto		
b. 1749	2 fl, orch		*Ricordi*
	2 fl, pf, arr.		*Andraud*

CLAPP, P.G. b. 1881	Prelude and Final wind quint		*Boosey & Hawkes*
CRAS, J. b. 1879	Quintet fl, vn, va, vc, harp		*Senart*
DAMASE, J.M. b. 1928	Quintet fl, vn, va, vc, harp		*Lemoine*
	17 Variations wind quint	Op. 22	*Leduc*
DANZI, F. b. 1763	2 Quintets wind quint	" 56, Nos. 1 and 2	*Chester*
DARKE, H. b. 1888	Meditation fl, strings		*O.U.P.*
DAVID, J.N. b. 1895	Divertimento wind quint, pf	" 24	*B. & H.*
DEMUTH, N. b. 1898	Concertino fl, strings		*Chester*
DÉSORMIÈRE, R. b. 1898	6 Danceries fl, cl, cor angl, fag, horn		*Leduc*
DIAMOND, D. b. 1915	Quintet fl, strings, pf		*Schirmer* *(C. Fisher)*
DITTERSORF, K.D. VON b. 1739	Concerto, E mi. fl, strings, clav		*Möseler*
DOUGLAS, R. b. 1907	6 Dance Caricatures wind quint		*Hinrichsen*
DRESDEN, S. b. 1881	3 Sextets wind quint, pf		*Donemus*
	Concerto fl, orch		"
DUBOIS, T. b. 1837	Au Jardin, Suite 2 fl, ob, 2 cl, horn, fag		*Heugel*
	Suite No. 1 2 fl, ob, 2 cl, horn, 2 fag		"
	Dixtuor wind quint, str quint		"
ELGAR, E. b. 1857	Nursery Suite, 2nd movements fl, orch		*Keith Prowse*
ENESCO, G. b. 1881	Dixtuor 2 fl, ob, cor angl, 2 cl, 2 fag, 2 horns		*Enoch (Paris)*
ERLEBACH, R.O. b. 1894	Rhapsody fl, ob (cor angl), vn, va, vc		*S. & B.*
ESCHER, R. b. 1912	'The Tomb of Ravel' fl, ob, vn, va, vc, harpsichord		*Donemus*

FALLA, M. DE b. 1876	Concerto pf, fl, ob, cl, vn, vc		*Eschig*
FERNANDEZ, O.L. 1948	Suite wind quint		*Assoc. Music Pub. (N.Y.)*
FINZI, G. b. 1901	A Severn Rhapsody fl, ob, 2 cl, horn, strings		*S. & B.*
FITELBERG, J. b. 1903	Capriccio fl, ob, cl, bass cl, tromb (or fag)		*Chester*
FLOTHIUS, M. b. 1914	Concerto fl, orch	Op. 19	*Donemus*
FOERSTER, J.B. b. 1859	Quintet wind quint Nonet wind quint, vn, va, vc, db	" 95 " 147	*Hudebni Matice (Artia)* " "
FOOTE, A.W. b. 1853	Night Piece fl, strings		*A.P. Schmidt (Boston)*
FRANÇAIX, J. b. 1912	2 Quintets wind quint fl, vn, va, vc, harp		*Schott* "
FREDERICK (THE GREAT) b. 1712	2 Concertos, Nos. 3 and 4 fl, strings, clav		*C.F. Vieweg (Musica Rara)*
FRICKER, P.R. b. 1920	Quintet wind quint	" 5	*Schott*
FRID, G. b. 1904	Serenade fl, 2 cl, fag, horn Nocturnes fl, harp, str quint	" 4 " 24	*Donemus* "
GAL, HANS b. 1890	Divertimento fl, ob, 2 cl, 2 horns, fag, trpt		*Leuckart*
GARDNER, J. b. 1917	Suite 2 fl (picc), 2 ob (cor angl), 2 cl (bass cl), 2 fag		*O.U.P.*
GENZMER, H. b. 1909	Septet fl, cl, horn, vn, va, vc, harp		*Schott*
GERHARD, R. b. 1896	Quintet wind quint		*Mills*
GERSTER, O. b. 1897	Quintet wind quint		*Schott*

GHEDINI, G.F. b. 1892	Works include: Concerto grosso wind quint, strings		*Zerboni*
	Concerto (L'Alderina) fl, vn, orch		*Ricordi*
GLUCK, C.W. b. 1714	Concerto, G ma. fl, strings, fl, pf, arr.		*Hug*
	Ballet Music from Alcestis 2 fl strings		*O.U.P.*
GOOSSENS, E. b. 1893	Phantasy fl, ob, 2 cl, 2 horns, 2 fag, trpt	Op. 40	*Curwen*
	3 pictures fl, strings, perc		*Chester*
GOUNOD, C.F. b. 1818	Petite Symphonie fl, 2 ob, 2 cl, 2 horns, 2 fag		*Costallat*
GRABNER, H. b. 1886	Suite fl, ob, cl, sax, horn, fag		*Kistner & Siegel*
	Concerto fl, cl, fag, horn, strings	Op. 48	" "
GRAENER, P. b. 1872	Suite fl, strings	" 63	*Z.*
GRAINGER, P.A. b. 1882	Walking Tune wind quint		*Schott*
GRAUPNER, C. b. 1683	Overture fl, 2 vn, va, clav		*Bärenreiter*
	Concerto, F ma. fl, strings, clav		*Schott*
GROOT, C. b. 1914	Concerto fl, orch		*Donemus*
HAMERIK, E. b. 1898	Quintet wind quint		*Samfundet*
HANDEL, G.F. b. 1685	Works include: 2 Concerti:		
	G mi. 2 fl, ob, 2 fag, strings, clav	Op. 3, No. 1	*B. & H.*
	F ma. fl, strings, clav	" 3, No. 4	*Schott*
	Mirtillo Suite fl, 2 ob, str quart, clav		*C.F. Kahnt*
HARSÁNYI, T. b. 1898	Nonet wind quint, str quart		*Eschig*

HASSE, J.A. b. 1699	Concerto, D ma. fl, strings, clav		*Eulenburg*
HAYDN, F.J.[1] b. 1732	Divertmenti: 2 in G ma. (Schmid) fl, 2 horns, strings		*Bärenreiter*
	D ma. (Scherchen) fl, strings		*Hug*
	B♭ ma. (Perry) wind quint, arr.		*Boosey & Hawkes*
	Notturni: C ma. (Schmid) fl, ob, 2 horns, strings		*Bärenreiter*
	C ma. (Schmid) 2 fl, 2 horns, string		*"*
	F ma. (Geiringer) fl, ob, 2 horns, strings		*U.E.*
HAUER, J. b. 1883	2 Dance Suites fl, ob, cl, fag, str quart, pf	Opp. 70, 71	*U.E.*
HENKEMANS, H. b. 1913	Concerto fl, orch		*Donemus*
	Quintet wind quint		*"*
HEINICHEN, J.D. b. 1683	Concerto grosso 2 fl, 2 ob, fag, strings, clav		*Eulenburg*
HENZE, H.W. b. 1926	Quintet wind quint		*Schott*
HILL, E.B. b. 1872	Sextet wind quint, pf	Op. 39	*Schirmer*
HINDEMITH, P.[2] b. 1895	Works include: Kleine Kammermusik wind quint	" 24, No. 2	*Schott*
	Septet fl, ob, cl, horn, trpt, bass cl, fag	" 43, No. 1	*"*
	Evening Concert fl, strings		*"*
	4 Pieces fl, trpt (or cl), strings		*"*

[1] A flute concerto in D ma., edited by Oskar Kaul and published by Leuckart, is sometimes attributed to Haydn.

[2] Several other works for strings and larger combinations of wind are published by Schott.

HINDEMITH, P.	Music		*Schott*
b. 1895 *(continued)*	2 fl, 2 ob, strings		
HÖFFDING, F.	Quintet	Op. 35	*S.M.*
b. 1899	wind quint		
HOLBROOKE, J.	Works include:		
b. 1878	4 Quintets		*Modern Music Library*
	wind quint		
	Sextet	,, ,, ,,	
	wind quint, pf		
	Nonet	,, ,, ,,	
	fl, ob, cl, fag, str		
	quint		
HÖLLER, K.	Divertimento	,, 11	*Willy Müller*
b. 1907	fl, vn, va, vc, pf		
HOLMBOE, V.	Quintet		*Musica Rara*
b. 1909	wind quint		
HOLST, G.	Fugal Concerto	,, 40, No. 2	*Novello*
b. 1874	fl, ob, strings		
	fl, pf, arr.		
HONEGGER, A.	Rhapsody		*Senart*
b. 1892	pf, 2 fl, cl		
	Concerto do Camera		*Salabert*
	fl, cor angl, strings		
HOWELLS, H.	Puck's Minuet		*Curwen*
b. 1892	2 fl, 2 cl, bass cl, pf,		
	perc		
HUMMEL, J.N.	2 Septets:		
b. 1778	Op. 74		*Peters*
	pf, fl, ob, horn, va,		
	vc, db		
	Op. 114 (The Military)		*Lienau*
	pf, fl, cl, trpt, vn,		
	vc, db		
IBERT, J.	3 Short Pieces		*Leduc*
b. 1890	wind quint		
	Capriccio		,,
	fl, ob, cl, fag, trpt,		
	harp, str quart		
D'INDY, V.	Suite	,, 24	*Hamelle*
b. 1851	2 fl, trpt, str quart		
	Sarabande et Menuet	,, 72 (from	,,
	wind quint, pf	Op. 24)	
	Chanson et Danses	,, 50	*Durand*
	fl, ob, 2 cl, horn, 2 fag		

D'INDY, V. b. 1851 (continued)	Concerto fl, vc, pf, strings Suite en parties fl, harp, va, vc	Op. 89 " 9·1	*Salabert* *Rouart Lerolle*
INGENHOVEN, J. b. 1876	Quintet wind quint		*Wunderhorn*
JACOB, G. b. 1895	Suite recorder, str quart		*O.U.P.*
JANÁČEK, L. b. 1854	2 Sextets wind quint, bass cl Suite wind quint, bass cl		*Chester* *Hudebni Matice* *(Artia)*
JOLIVET, A. b. 1905	Chant de Linos fl (solo), vn, va, vc, harp or pf Serenade wind quint Concerto fl, strings		*Leduc* *Costallat* *U.M.P.*
JONGEN, J. b. 1873	Preamble and Dances wind quint Concerto wind quint Rhapsodie wind quint, pf	Op. 98 " 124 " 70	*Andraud* " "
JUON, P. b. 1872	Divertimento pf, wind quint	" 51	*Lienau*
KARG-ELERT, S. b. 1879	Quintet wind quint	" 30	*Musica Rara*
KAUFFMANN, L.J. b. 1901	Quintet wind quint		*U.E.*
KLUGHARDT, A. b. 1847	Quintet wind quint	" 79	*Doblinger*
KOECHLIN, C. b. 1867	Primavera fl, vn, va, vc, harp Septet wind quint, cor angl, sax		*Senart* *L'Oiseau Lyre*
KOPPEL, H.D. b. 1908	Sextet wind quint, pf	Op. 36	*S.M.*
KORNAUTH, E. b. 1891	Nonet fl, ob, cl, horn, str quint	" 31	*U.E.*
KRENEK, E. b. 1900	Concertino fl, vn, harpsichord, strings Symphonic Music for 9 solo instruments fl, ob, cl, fag, string quint	" 27	" "

KRENEK, E. b. 1900 *(continued)*	Concerto grosso fl, cl, fag, vn, va, vc, orch	Op. 10	*U.E.*
LAJTHA, L. b. 1892	Marionettes fl, vn, va, vc, harp	" 26	*Chester*
	Quintet fl, vn, va, vc, harp	" 46	*Otto Junne (Munich)*
	Voyage fl, vn, va, vc, harp	" "
LADMIRAULT, P.E. b. 1877	Choral et Variations wind quint, pf		*Leduc*
LANDRÉ, G. b. 1905	Quintet wind quint		*Donemus*
	Symphonic Music fl, orch		"
LEFÈBVRE, C.E. b. 1843	Suite wind quint	" 57	*Hamelle*
LEIBOWITZ, R. b. 1913	Nonet wind quint, vn, va, vc, db	" 10	*U.E.*
LILIEN, I. b. 1897	Sonatine double wind quint		*Donemus*
	Concertino 2 fl, orch		"
LOEILLET, J.B. b. 1653	Quintet, B mi. 2 fl, 2 recorders, clav		*Bärenreiter*
LUENING, O. b. 1900	Fuguing Tune wind quint		*Assoc. Music Pub. (N.Y.)*
MAGNARD, A. b. 1865	Quintet pf, fl, ob, cl, fag	" 8	*Rouart Lerolle*
MALIPIERO, G.F. b. 1882	Sonata fl, vn, va, vc, harp		*Ricordi*
	Ricercare and Ritrovari wind quint, 4 va, vc, db		"
	Dialoghi No. 4 wind quint		"
MARTINU, B. b. 1890	Quintet wind quint		*Chester*
MARX, K. b. 1899	Divertimento fl, vn, va, vc, pf		*Bärenreiter*
	Variations fl, 2 recorders, ob, va, vc		"
MASON, D.G. b. 1873	3 Pieces fl, harp, str quart	Op. 13	*Schirmer (C. Fisher)*

MATHIAS, W.	Quintet		MS.
b. 1934			
MEALE, R.	Plateau		U.E.
b. 1932	Quintet		"
MIGOT, G.	Quintet		U.M.P.
b. 1891	wind quint		
MILFORD, R.	Suite		O.U.P.
b. 1903	fl, strings (sop ad lib)		
MILHAUD, D.	Works include:		
b. 1892	La Cheminée du Roi René		Andraud
	wind quint		
	Sérénade		U.E.
	fl, cl, fag, vn, va, vc, db		
	Pastorale		"
	fl, cor angl, fag, vn, va, vc, db		
	Dixtuor		"
	fl, picc, ob, cor angl, cl, bass cl, 2 fag, 2 horns		
MORITZ, E.	Quintet	Op. 41	Z.
b. 1891	wind quint		
MOZART, W.A.	3 Divertimenti		B. & H.
b. 1756	K 131		
	fl, ob, fag, 4 horns, str quint		
	K 187		
	2 fl, 5 trpt, 4 drums		
	K 188		
	2 fl, 6 trpt, 4 drums		
	3 Concertos[1]		"
	K 299, C ma.		
	fl, harp, orch		
	fl, pf, arr.		
	K 313, G ma.		
	fl, orch		
	fl, pf, arr.		
	K 314, D ma.		
	fl, orch		
	fl, pf, arr.		
	Andante, C ma. K 315		"
	fl, orch		
	fl, pf, arr.		

[1]Cadenzas to the concertos are included in Section 2.

MOZART, W.A. b. 1756 (continued)	Adagio and Rondo, K 617 glass harmonica (or pf), fl, ob, va, vc		*Doblinger*
	5 Country Dances, K 609 fl, strings, side drum		*Peters*
	Adagio and Allegro, K 594 (arr. Spiegl) fl, ob, 2 cl, fag, vn, va		*O.U.P.*
	Fantasy K 608 (arr. Pijper) wind quint, pf		*Donemus*
MULDER, E.W. b. 1898	Sextet wind quint, pf		"
MÜLLER, P. b. 1898	3 Quintets wind quint		*Rühle*
NIELSEN, C. b. 1865	Quintet wind quint	Op. 43	*Hansen*
	Concerto fl, orch		*Dannia* *(Musica Rara)*
NOETEL, K.F. b. 1903	Concertino fl, vn, strings		*Bärenreiter*
NUSSIO, O. b. 1902	Bagatellen fl, vn, (oblig), strings		*Z.*
	fl, pf, arr.		"
ONSLOW, G. b. 1783	Works include: Quintet wind quint	" 81	*B. & H.* *(Musica Rara)*
OSIECK, H. b. 1910	Divertimento wind quint, pf		*Donemus*
PERSICHETTI, V. b. 1915	Pastoral wind quint	" 21	*Schirmer*
PESSARD, E.L.F. b. 1843	Aubade wind quint	" 6	*Leduc*
PEZ, J.C. b. 1664	Concerto Pastorale 2 fl, strings		*C.F. Vieweg* *(Musica Rara)*
PFEIFFER, G.J. b. 1835	Sonata fl, ob, fag, horn, harp- sichord		*Chester*
PIERNÉ, G. b. 1863	Pastorale wind quint	" 14, No. 1	*Leduc*
	Voyage fl, vn, va, vc, harp		*Leduc*

PIERNÉ, G.	Variations Libres et		*Salabert*
b. 1863	Final		
(continued)	fl, vn, va, vc, harp		
	Prelude and Fugue	Op. 40, No. 1	*Hamelle*
	2 fl, ob, cl, 2 fag, horn		
	Pastorale variée	" 30	*Durand*
	fl, ob, cl, horn, trpt, 2 fag		
PISTON, W.	Quintet		*Assoc. Music Pub.*
b. 1894	fl, str quart		*(N.Y.)*
	Divertimento	" " "
	fl, ob, cl, fag, str quart, db		
POULENC, F.	Rhapsodie Nègre		*Chester*
b. 1899	fl, cl, str quart, voice (ad lib), pf		
	Sextet		*Hansen*
	wind quint, pf		
	Mouvements Perpetuels		*Chester*
	wind quint, cor angl, strings		
PIJPER, W.	Quintet		*Donemus*
b. 1894	wind quint		"
	Sextet		
	wind quint, pf		"
	Septet		
	wind quint, db, pf		
QUANTZ, J.J.	Works include:		
b. 1697	Concertos:		
	fl, strings, clav		
	D ma.		*Möseler*
	fl, pf, arr.		*Andraud*
	G ma.		*Musica Rara*
	fl, pf, arr.		*B. & H.*
	C ma.		*Möseler*
RATHAUS, K.	Serenade		*Boosey & Hawkes*
b. 1905	wind quint		
RAVEL, M.	Introduction and Allegro		*Durand*
	fl, cl, harp, str quart		
RAWSTHORNE, A.	Concertante Pastoral		*O.U.P.*
b. 1905	fl, horn, strings		
REICHA, A.	2 Quintets		
b. 1770	wind quint	Op. 88, No. 2	*Doblinger*
	wind quint	" 98. No. 3	*Hofmeister*

REINECKE, C.H.C. b. 1824	Sextet fl, ob, cl, 2 horns fag	Op. 271	Z.
	Ballade fl, orch	" 288	(Musica Rara)
REIZENSTEIN, F. b. 1911	Quintet wind quint		Boosey & Hawkes
RHENÉ-BATON b. 1879	Aubade fl, ob, 2 cl, horn, 2 fag	" 53	Durand
RIEGGER, W. b. 1885	Quintet wind quint	" 51	Schott
	Concerto wind quint, pf	" 53	Assoc. Mus. Pub. (N.Y.)
RIETI, V. b. 1898	Concerto wind quint, orch		U.E.
RIVIER, J. b. 1896	Concerto fl, strings		Noel (U.M.P.)
ROGERS, B. b. 1893	Fantasy fl, va, orch		Elkan Vogel
	Soliloquy fl, orch		C. Fisher
RÖNTGEN, J. b. 1855	Serenade fl, ob, cl, 2 horns, 2 fag	" 14	B. & H.
ROOS, R. DE b. 1907	Sextet wind quint, pf		Donemus
	Dances fl, orch		"
ROPARTZ, J.G. b. 1864	Prelude, Marine et Chanson fl, harp, vn, va, vc		Durand
	Deux Pièces wind quint		"
ROTA, N. b. 1911	Quintet fl, ob, va, vc, harp		Ricordi
ROUSSEL, A.C.P. b. 1869	Divertissement pf, wind quint	" 6	Rouart Lerolle
	Sérénade harp, fl, vn, va, vc	" 30	" "
RUBBRA, E. b. 1901	Suite (The Buddha) fl, ob, vn, va, vc	" 64	Lengnick
	Fantasia recorder (fl), str quart, harpsichord		"
RUYNEMAN, D. b. 1886	Quintet wind quint		Donemus
SALVIUCCI, G. b. 1907	Serenate fl, ob, cl, trpt, fag, str quart		Ricordi

SAUGUET, H.	5 Pieces		*Rouart Lerolle*
b. 1901	fl, cl, vn, fag, pf		
	Divertissement		*Eschig*
	fl, cl va, fag, pf		
	'Pres du Bal'		*Otto Junne*
	fl, cl, vn, fag, pf		*(Munich)*
SCARLATTI, A.	2 Sinfonia		*Schott*
b. 1659	fl, string quart, clav		
SCHMID, H.K.	Quintet	Op. 28	"
b. 1874	wind quint		
SCHMITT, F.	Rococo Suite	" 84	*Durand*
b. 1870	fl, harp, vn, va, vc		
	Chants Alizés		"
	wind quint		
	Lied and Scherzo		"
	double wind quint		
SCHOECK, O.	Sérénade	" 1	*Chester*
b. 1886	wind quint, str quart		
SCHÖNBERG, A.	Quintet	" 26	*U.E.*
b. 1874	wind quint		
	Chamber Symphony	" 9	"
	(arr. Webern)		
	fl, cl, vn, va, vc, pf		
SCHULTZ, S.S.	Quintet		*Chester*
b. 1913	wind quint		
SEIBER, M.	Fantasy		*Zerboni*
b. 1905	fl, horn, str quart		
SIBELIUS, J.	Suite mignonne	" 98a	*Fürstner*
b. 1865	2 fl, 2 vn, va, vc, db		*(Musica Rara)*
SIEGEL, O.	Concerto		*Z.*
b. 1896	fl, strings		
SMIT, L.	Quintet		*Donemus*
b. 1900	fl, vn, va, vc, harp		
	Sextet		"
	wind quint, pf		
SPELMAN, T.M.	Poème		*Chester*
b. 1891	fl, vn, va, vc, harp		
SPOHR, L.	Nonet	Op. 31	*Litolff*
b. 1784	wind quint, vn, va,		
	vc, db		
	Quintet	" 52	*Doblinger*
	fl, cl, horn, fag, pf		
STAMITZ, C.	Concerto		*Z.*
b. 1745	fl, strings		
	Sinfonie E♭ ma.		*C.F. Vieweg*
	2 fl, 2 horns, strings		*(Musica Rara)*

STANFORD, C.V.	Serenade	Op. 95	*S. & B.*
b. 1852	fl, cl, horn, 2 fag, str		
STOCKHAUSEN, K.	Zeitmasse		*U.E.*
b. 1928			
STOKER, R.	Quintet		*Hinrichsen*
b. 1938			
STRATEGIER, H.	Concerto		*Donemus*
b. 1912	fl, orch		
STRAUSS, R.	Serenade	" 7	*U.E.*
b. 1864	2 fl, 2 ob, 2 cl, 4 horns,		
	2 fag, 2 contra fag		
STRAVINSKY, I.	Octet		*E.R.*
b. 1882	fl, cl, 2 trpt, 2 fag, 2 tromb		
SZALOWSKI, A.	Concertino		
b. 1907	fl, strings		*Amphion*
	fl, pf, arr.		*U.M.P.*
	Quintet		*Omega*
	wind quint		
TAILLEFERRE, G.	Images		*Chester*
b. 1892	fl, cl, str quart, celeste, pf		
TANSMAN, A.	Danse from 'Le Jardin		*Schott*
b. 1897	du Paradis'		
	wind quint, pf		
TARP, S.E.	Serenade		*Samfundet*
b. 1908	fl, cl, vn, va, vc		*(Chester)*
	Concertino	.	"
	fl, orch		
TELEMANN, G.P.	Works include:		
b. 1681	Suite, A mi.		*Hinrichsen*
	fl, strings, clav		
	fl, pf, arr.		
	Concertos:		
	B♭ ma.		*Möseler*
	2 fl, strings, clav		
	A mi.		*Nagel*
	2 fl, strings, clav		
	E mi.		*Bärenreiter*
	fl, recorder, 2 vn, va, clav		
	E ma.		*Hinrichsen*
	fl, ob, d'amore, va		
	d'amore, strings, clav		
	F ma.		*Möseler*
	fl, strings, clav		
	C ma.		*C.F. Vieweg*
	2 fl, strings		*(Musica Rara)*

THUILLE, L. b. 1861	Sextet wind quint, pf	Op. 6	*Doblinger*
TOMASI, H. b. 1901	Variations wind quint		*Leduc*
TOVEY, D. F. b. 1875	Variations on a theme by Gluck fl, str quart		*Schott*
VACTOR, D. VAN b. 1906	Quintet fl, str quart		*Schirmer (C. Fisher)*
VALEN, F. b. 1887	Serenade wind quint	" 42	• *Lyche*
VARÈSE, E. b. 1885	Octet wind quint, trpt, tromb, db		*Ricordi*
VAUGHAN WILLIAMS, R. b. 1872	Fantasia on 'Green-sleeves' (arr. Greaves) 2 fl, strings, harp		*O.U.P.*
VEALE, J. b. 1922	Elegy fl, strings, harp		*O.U.P.*
VILLA LOBOS, H. b. 1887	Quintet fl, ob, cor angl, cl, fag Choros, No. 7 fl, ob, cl, sax, fag, vn, pf		*Schott* "
VOGEL, V. b. 1896	Ticinella fl, ob, cl, sax, fag		"
VIVALDI, A b. 1680	Works include: [1] 6 Concertos (Mali-piero) fl, ob, vn, fag, clav 7 Concertos (Mali-piero) fl, strings, clav 3 Concertos (Mali-piero) picc, strings, clav		*Ricordi* " "
WAGENER-RÉGENY, R. b. 1903	Divertimento fl, cl, fag, perc		*B. & H.*
WAILLY, P. DE b. 1854	Octet fl, ob, 2 cl, 2 fag, horn, trpt		*Rouart Lerolle*

[1]Other Concertos (ed. G. F. Malipiero) may be found in the lists published by Ricordi in conjunction with the Vivaldi Institute of Treviso.

WEBERN, A.	Concerto fl, ob, cl, horn, trpt, tromb, vn, va, pf	Op. 24	*U.E.*
WEIS, F. b. 1898	Serenade wind quint		*Hansen*
WELLESZ, E. b. 1885	Suite wind quint	" 73	*Sikorsky*
	Pastorale fl, ob, sax, trpt, perc, strings		*U.E.*
WHITE, F.H. b. 1884	4 Proverbs fl, ob, vn, va, vc		*S. & B.*
WISHART, P.C.A. b. 1921	Aubade fl, strings		*Hinrichsen*
	fl, str quart		*"*
WOLF-FERRARI, E. b. 1876	Chamber Symphony pf, wind quint, str quart, db	" 8	*Rahter*
ZAGWIJN, H. b. 1878	Quintet wind quint		*Donemus*
	Suite wind quint, pf		*"*
	Scherzo fl, ob, vn, va, vc, pf		*"*
	Entracte and Fugue fl, ob, vn, va, vc, pf		*"*
	Nocturne fl, cor angl, cl, fag, horn, harp, celeste		*"*
	Concerto fl, orch		*"*
ZECCHI, A. b. 1904	Divertimento fl, harp, strings		*Bongiovanni*
ZILCHER, H. b. 1881	Quintet wind quint	" 90	*Willy Müller*

4. VOICE AND FLUTE, & C.

ALABIEFF, A.A. b. 1787	The Russian Nightingale sop, fl, pf		*Chappell*
ANDERS, E. b. 1883	Flötenlieder sop, fl, pf	Op. 109	*Z.*

APOSTEL, H.E.	5 Songs	Op. 22	*U.E.*
b. 1901	med voice, fl, cl, fag		
ARNE, T.A.	Cantata		*Schott*
b. 1710	sop, fl, pf (strings ad lib)		
BACH, J.S.[1]	Works include:		
b. 1685	Duet: No. 7 (Mass in B mi.)		*B. & H.*
	sop, ten, fl, strings, clav		
	Arias:		*B. & H.*
	No. 58 (St. Matthew) Passion)		
	sop, fl, 2 ob da caccia		
	No. 13 (St. John Passion)		
	sop, fl, strings, clav		
	No. 63 (St. John Passion)		
	sop, 2 fl (unis.), 2 ob da caccia (unis.)		
BANTOCK, G.	3 Songs		*Swan*
b. 1868	sop, fl		
	3 Idylls		*Cramer*
	contralto, fl (vc, ad lib)		
BAX, A.	'I heard a piper piping'		*Chappell*
b. 1883	sop, fl, pf		
BECK, C.	Cantata		*Schott*
b. 1901	sop, fl, strings, pf		
BEDFORD, H.	Night Piece No. 2		*S. & B.*
b. 1867	voice, fl, ob, pf		
BENEDICT, J.	Song		*Boosey & Hawkes*
b. 1804	voice, fl, pf		
BENJAMIN, A.	'The Piper'		*Elkin*
b. 1893	sop, fl, pf		

[1]The Cantatas and Oratorios (B. & H.) include many numbers for voice with obbligati for flute or flutes: Nos. 8, 11, 13, 18, 26, 30, 34, 39, 45, 46, 78, 81, 94, 96, 99, 100, 102, 103, 106, 107, 113, 114, 115, 177, 119, 122, 123, 129, 130, 142, 157, 161, 164, 173, 175, 180, 182, 184, 191, 201, 205, 206, 209, 211. Christmas Oratorio (part 3), The Easter Oratorio.

BISHOP, H. R. b. 1876	'Lo, here the gentle lark' voice, fl, pf		*Elkin*
BLISS, A. b. 1891	Rout sop, fl, cl, str quart, bass, gl, s.d.		*Curwen*
	Madam Noy sop, fl, cl, va, cb, fag, harp		*Chester*
	Rhapsody sop, ten, fl, cor angl, strings		*S. & B.*
	Pastorale sop, chorus, fl, strings, timp		*Novello*
	5 Songs voice, fl, ob, cl, strings, perc		*Chester*
BONNER, E. b. 1889	Flutes (4 Songs) med voice, fl, cl, fag, harp (or pf)		*"*
BRAND, M. b. 1896	5 Songs sop, fl, ob, cl, horn, vn, vc		*U.E.*
BRESGEN, G b. 1913	2 Folk Songs voices, 2 fl, pf		*Schott*
CALDARA, A. b. 1670	'Quell' Usignuolo' (van Leeuwen) sop, fl, clav		*Z.*
CHAMINADE, C. b. 1861	Portrait voice, fl, pf		*Enoch (Paris)*
COPLAND, A. b. 1900	'As it fell upon a day' voice, fl, cl		*Boosey & Hawkes (N.Y.)*
COUPERIN, F. b. 1668	Motet sop, fl, vns, organ		*L'Oiseau Lyre*
DELIBES, L. b. 1836	'Le Rossignol' voice, fl, pf		*Z.*
DUREY, L. b. 1888	'Images à Crusoe' voice, fl, cl, str quart, celeste		*Chester*
EISLER, H. b. 1898	Palmström speaker, fl, cl, vn, vc	Op. 5	*U.E.*
FALLA, M. DE b. 1876	Psyché voice, fl, cl, vn, vc	" 5	*Schott*

FLOTHUIS, M.	Cantata	Óp. 34	*Donemus*
b. 1914	contralto, fl, ob d'amore, va, vc		
GÁL, HANS	Nachtmusik		*A. Robitschek*
b. 1890	sop, chorus, fl, vc, pf		*(Vienna)*
GAUBERT, P.	Song		*Enoch (Paris)*
b. 1879	voice, fl, pf		
GERHARD, R.	5 Songs		*Keith Prowse*
b. 1896	sop, fl, pf		
GRÉTRY, A.E.M.	Recit. and Air		*Z.*
b. 1741	(van Leeuwen) sop, fl, clav		
HANDEL, G.F.[1]	Works include:		
b. 1685	Cantata, 'Nel dolce dell'oblio'		*"*
	sop, fl, clav		
	Air du Rossignol (L'Allegro)		*Lemoine*
	sop, fl, clav		
	Aria (Acis and Galatea)		*Schott*
	sop, fl, clav		
	2 Arias •		*Novello*
	sop, fl, clav		
HINDEMITH, P.	6 Poems	Op. 23, No. 2	*Schott*
b. 1895	contralto, fl, cl, strings		
HOLST, G.	Works include:		
b. 1874	'Savitri' (Chamber Opera) voices, double str quart, db, 2 fl, cor angl		*Curwen*
HONEGGER, A.	3 Songs		*Senart*
b. 1892	voice, fl, str quart		
IBERT, J.	2 Songs		*Otto Junne*
b. 1890	sop, fl		*(Munich)*
KNAB, A.	2 Cantatas		*Schott*
b. 1881	sop, fl, strings		
KRENEK, E.	Works include:		
b. 1900	'The Nightingale'	Op. 68	*U.E.*
	sop, 2 fl, strings		
LAMBERT, C.	7 Poems		*Chester*
b. 1905	voice, fl, ob, cl, strings		

[1]The Operas and Cantatas include many numbers for solo voice with obbligati for fl.

MARX, J. b. 1882	'Pan trauert um Syrinx' voice, fl, pf	*U.E.*
MARX, K. b. 1897	Cantata alto, fl, vn, vc, pf	*Bärenreiter*
MASSÉ, V. b. 1822	The Nightingale's Song sop, fl	*Lienau*
MILFORD, R. b. 1903	'Go, little book' sop, fl, strings	*O.U.P.*
MILHAUD, D. b. 1892	6 Songs voice, fl, cl, fag, vn, va, vc, db	*U.E.*
ORR, R. b. 1909	3 Pastorals sop, fl, va, pf	*Hinrichsen*
ORREGO, S.J. b. 1919	5 Canciones Castellanas voice, fl, cor angl, cl, horn, harp, perc	*Chester*
PAISIELLO, G. b. 1741	Aria sop, fl, pf	*Schott*
PEPUSCH, J.C. b. 1667	Cantata sop, fl, pf	*U.E.*
PETYREK, F. b. 1892	'Das heilige Abendmahl' voices, fl, va, vc, db, organ	*,,*
PURCELL, H. b. 1658	3 Cantatas 'Hark, Damon, hark' 2 sop bass, 2 fl, strings, clav 'We reap all the plea- sures' sop, ten, bass, 2 fl, clav 'When night her purple veil' barit, 2 fl, clav Song sop, 2 fl, pf	*Novello* *Schott*
RAMEAU, J.P. b. 1683	'Rossignols amoureux' sop, fl, clav	*Lemoine*
RAVEL, M. b. 1875	3 Poems of Mallarmé voice, pf, str quart, 2 fl, 2 cl	*Durand*
RAWSTHORNE, A. b. 1905	'A Canticle of Man. barit, chorus, fl, strings (or pf)	*O.U.P.*

REUTTER, H. b. 1900	Lyrische Konzert mezzo sop, fl, strings, pf	Op. 70	*Schott*
RICCIO, T. b. 1540	'Jubilent omnes' sop, fl, vn, fag, clav		*Nagel*
ROLAND-MANUEL, A. b, 1891	Deux Elegies sop, fl		*Otto Junne (Munich)*
ROUSSEL, A.C.P. b. 1869	Deux Poèmes voice, fl	Op. 26	"
SCARLATTI, A. b. 1659	Cantata (van Leeuwen) sop, fl, clav		*Z.*
SCHOECK, O. b. 1886	Suite: 'Gaselen' barit, pf, fl, ob, bass cl, trpt, perc	" 38	*B. & H.*
SCHÖNBERG, A. b. 1874	'Pierrot Lunaire' reciter, pf, fl, cl, vn, vc	" 21	*U.E.*
SCOTT, C. b. 1879	Idyll voice, fl		*Elkin*
SEARLE, H. b. 1915	'Put away the flutes' high voice, fl, ob, str quart	" 11	*Lengnick*
	'The Owl and the Pussy Cat' speaker, fl (picc), guitar, vc		*O.U.P.*
	'Two Practical Cats' speaker, fl (picc), guitar, vc		"
SMYTH, E.M. b. 1858	4 Songs voice, fl, strings, perc		*Novello*
STRAVINSKY, I. b. 1882	Pribaoutki voice, fl, ob, cl, fag, str quart		*Chester*
	Trois Poésies voice, pf, fl, cl, str quart		*E.R.*
	4 Songs sop, fl, harp, guitar		*Chester*
	3 Shakespeare Songs contralto, fl, cl, va		*Boosey & Hawkes*

TELEMANN, G.P.[1]	Works include:	
b. 1681	2 Cantatas	*Bärenreiter*
	voice, fl, clav	
	voice, 2 fl, va, clav	
	Aria (Ermlet)	*Z.*
	voice, fl, clav (vc ad lib)	
TULOU, J.H.	Chanson	*Lemoine*
b. 1786	voice, pf, fl	
VAUGHAN	The Bridal Day	*O.U.P.*
WILLIAMS, R.	speaker, barit, chorus,	
b. 1872	fl, strings, pf	
	Epithalamion	*"*
	barit, chorus, fl (picc), strings, pf	
VERDI, G.	Nocturne	*Ricordi*
b. 1813	3 voices, fl, pf	
VILLA-LOBOS, H.	Works include:	
b. 1887	Quartet	*Schott*
	chorus, fl, sax, harp, celeste	
	Poêma	*"*
	voice, fl, cl, pf	
WALTON, W.T.	Façade	*O.U.P.*
b. 1902	reciter, fl, cl, sax, trpt, vc, perc	
WARLOCK, P.	The Curlew	*S. &.B.*
b. 1894	tenor, fl, cor angl, str quart	
WEBERN, A.VON	5 Sacred Songs Op. 15	*U.E.*
b. 1883	sop, fl, vn, cl, trpt, harp	
WEILL, E.	Frauentanz " 10	*"*
b. 1900	sop, fl, va, cl, horn, fag	

5. FLUTE OR FLUTES WITH OTHER INSTRUMENTS

ADDISON, J.	Trio	*Augener*
b. 1920	fl, ob, pf	

[1] 72 Church Cantatas for voice, and a melody instrument (fl, recorder, ob or vn) are published by Bärenreiter.

ALBINONI, T. b. 1671	Concerto G ma. (str. O)		*Ricordi*
AMBROSIUS, H. b. 1897	Concerto (O)		*Erdmann*
ANDERSEN, K. b. 1847	2 Trios fl, cl, vc fl, vn, va	Op. 5 ,, 15	*Nordiska* *Chester*
ANDRIESSEN, H. b. 1892	Theme and Variations fl, ob, pf Intermezzo fl, harp Pastorale fl, vn, pf		*Donemus* ,, ,, ,,
ANDRIEESEN, J. b. 1925	Trio fl, ob, pf Suite de Nöel fl, vn, va, pf		,,
APOSTEL, H.E. b. 1901	5 Bagatelles fl, cl, fag Quartet fl, cl, horn, fag	Op. 20 ,, 14	*U.E.* ,,
ARNOLD, M. b. 1921	Divertimento fl, ob, cl Trio fl, va, fag	,, 37	*Paterson* ,,
ARRIEU, C. b. 1903	Concerto fl, pf (P) Wind Quintet		*Amphion* *U.M.P.*
BACH, C.P.E. b. 1714	2 Duets fl, vn Trios fl, vn, clav B♭ ma. B mi. 12 Kleine Stücke fl, vn, clav 3 Quartets, C ma. D ma. G ma. fl, va, vc, clav		*Nagel* ,, *Hinrichsen* *Doblinger* *Z.* *Doblinger*
BACH, J.C. b. 1735	Concerto, G ma. (Spiegl) (str. O) Concerto in D Quartets fl, vn, va, vc		*Schott* *U.E.*

BACH, J.C.		Op. 8, No.1	*Hinrichsen*
b. 1735		" 8, No.4	*Nagel*
(continued)	Quartet	" 20, No.2	
	2 fl, va, vc		*Bärenreiter*
BACH, J.C.F.	Trio, C ma.		*Kistner & Siegel*
b. 1732	fl, vn, clav		
BACH, J.S.	Trio Sonatas		*Peters*
b. 1685	G ma. C mi.		
	fl, vn, clav		
	G ma.		*B. & H.*
	2 fl, clav		
	7 Inventions (arr.)		*Hinrichsen*
	fl, cl, fag		
BACH, W.F.	3 Trios		*B. & H.*
b. 1710	2 fl, clav		
	Trio		*Bärenreiter*
	2 fl, va		
	Sonata, B♭ ma.		*B. & H.*
	fl, vn, clav		
BADINGS, H.	Ballade		*Donemus*
b 1907	fl, harp		
BARRAUD, H.	Flute Concerto		*Boosey & Hawkes*
b. 1900			
BAX, A.	Elegiac Trio		*Chester*
b. 1883	fl, va, harp		
BECK, C.	Sonatine		*Eschig*
b. 1901	fl, vn		
BEETHOVEN,	Serenade	Op. 25	*Peters*
L. VAN. b. 1770	fl, vn, va		
BENNETT, R.R.	Trio		*U.E.*
b. 1936	fl, ob, cl		
BENTZON, J.	Sonatine	Op. 7	*S.M.*
b. 1897	fl, cl, fag		
	Racconto	" 25, No. 1	"
	fl, sax, fag, db		
	Racconto	" 30	*Chester*
	fl, vn, va, vc		
BENTZON, N.V.	Mosaique Musicale	" 54	*Nordiska*
b. 1919	fl, vn, vc, pf		
BERIO, L.	Serenata		*Zerboni*
b. 1925	fl (+ 14 instruments)		
	Differences		*U.E.*
	fl, cl, harp, va, vc, tape		
	Tempi Concertati		"
	fl, vn, 2 pfs + 4 ensembles		

BERKELEY, LENNOX, b. 1903	Concertino recorder (fl), vn, vc, harpsichord	Op. 48	*Chester*
BIRTWISTLE, H. b. 1934	Cantata sop, fl/picc, cl, vn/va, vc, pf/cel, glock		*U.E.*
BLACHER, B. b. 1903	Divertimento fl, ob, cl, fag	Op. 38	*Doblinger*
BLAVET, M. b. 1700	Concerto, A mi. (str O)		*Ricordi*
BOUGHTON, R. b. 1871	Concerto (str O)		*Boosey & Hawkes*
BOCCHERINI, L. b. 1743	Flute Concerto		*Southern*
BOISMORTIER, J.B. DE b. 1691	Concerto, C ma. fl, ob, clav		*Ricordi*
BOULEZ, P. b. 1925	Marteau sans Maitre alto fl, mezzo sop, guitar, vn, vibraphone, marimbaphone, perc		*U.E.*
BOZZA, E. b. 1905	Sonatine fl, fag		*Leduc*
BRIDGE. F. b. 1879	Divertimenti fl, ob, cl, fag		*Boosey & Hawkes*
BROWN, E. b. 1926	Times 5 fl, cl, trpt, tmb, 2 vns, va, vc, pf		*U.E.*
BURKHARD, W. b. 1900	Serenade fl, cl		*Bärenreiter*
	Serenade fl, guitar	Op. 71, No.3	*Doblinger*
	Lyrische Musik fl, vn, vc, pf		*Bärenreiter*
BUTTING, M. b. 1888	Concerto (O)		*Peters*
BUXTEHUDE, D. b. 1637	Sonata fl, vc, clav		*Schott*
CARTAN, J. b. 1906	Sonatine fl, cl		*Heugel*
CARTER, E.C. b. 1908	Quartet fl, ob, vc, harpsichord		*Assoc. Music Pub. (NY)*
CARULLI, F. b. 1770	2 Notturni, A mi. C ma. fl, vn, guitar		*Doblinger*
	5 Serenades fl, guitar		*"*

CASADESUS, R b. 1899	Concerto (O)	Op. 35	*Andraud*
CASTERA, R. DE b. 1873	Concert pf, fl, vc, cl		*Rouart*
CORELLI, A b. 1653	Sonatas arr. 2 fl, vc, clav	Op. 2, Nos. 1, *Br. Mus. L.* 5, 7	
CORRETTE, M. b. 1709	Suite, C ma. fl, vn, clav		*Ricordi*
COUPERIN, F. b. 1668	2 Concerts, Nos. 4 and 9 fl, vc, clav		*L'Oiseau Lyre*
	Concert No. 6 (str O)		*Delrieu (Nice)*
CRAS, J. b. 1879	Suite fl, harp		*Senart*
DAMASE, J.M. b. 1928	Sonata fl, vc, pf	" 17	*Lemoine*
	Trio fl, vc, harp		*"*
DAVID, J.N. b. 1895	Sonata fl, va	" 32, No. 1	*B. & H.*
	Variations fl, lute	.. 32, No. 2	*"*
	Sonata fl, va, guitar	" 26	*"*
	Trio fl, vn, va	" 30	*"*
DAVIES, P.M. b. 1934	Alma Redemptoris Mater fl, ob, 2 cls, fag, horn		*Schott*
	Ricercare and Doubles on 'To Many a Well' fl, ob, cl, fag, horn, va, vc, harpsichord		*"*
DEBUSSY, C.A. b. 1862	Sonata fl, va, harp		*Durand*
DOUGLAS, R. b. 1907	Trio fl, vn, va		*Hinrichsen*
	2 Quartets fl, vn, va, harp		*"*
DUBOIS, T. b. 1837	Terzettino fl, va, harp		*Heugel*
DUKELSKY, V. b. 1903	Trio fl, fag, pf		*E. R.*
DUNHILL, T.F. b. 1877	2 Short Pieces fl, vn, va, pf		*Augener*
DUPIN, P. b. 1865	Pièces Dialoguées No. 1 fl, vc, harp		*Durand*

DURUFLÉ, M. b. 1902	Prélude, Récit et Variations fl, va, pf	Op. 3	"
DUSSEK, J.L. b. 1761	2 Trios fl, vc, pf	Opp. 21,65	*B. & H.*
EMMANUEL, M. b. 1862	Trio Sonata pf, fl, cl		*Lemoine*
FIALA, J. b. 1748	Duo fl, fag		*Schmidt*
FINGER, G. b. 1660	Sonata, D mi. fl, ob, pf		*Chester*
FLOTHIUS, M. b. 1914	Nocturne fl, ob, cl	Op. 11	*Donemus*
FORTNER, W. b. 1907	Serenade fl, ob, fag		*Schott*
FRANÇAIX, J. b. 1912	Musique de Cour fl, vn, pf		"
	Quartet fl, ob, cl, fag		"
FRICKER, P.R. b. 1920	Octet, fl, cl, horn, fag, vn, va, vc, db	Op. 30	"
FUKUSHIMA, K. b. 1930	Hi-Kio alto fl, strings, perc		*Zerboni*
FUX, J.J. b. 1660	Sinfonia fl, ob, clav		*Nagel*
FURSTNEAU, K. b. 1772	12 Pieces fl, guitar		"
GÁL, HANS b. 1890	Suite fl, 2 vn		*M. & H.* *Publications Inc.*
GALLON, NOËL b. 1878	Sonata fl, fag		*Leduc*
GASSMANN, F. b. 1729	6 Trios fl, vn, va		*Kistner & Siegel*
GAUBERT, P. b. 1879	Tarantella fl, ob, pf		*Enoch (Paris)*
GILSE, J. VAN b. 1881	Trio fl, vn, va		*Alsbach*
GOEHR, A b. 1932	Suite fl, cl, horn, harp, vn/va, vc	Op. 11	*Schott*
GOEPFART, K.E. b. 1859	Quartet fl, ob, cl, fag		*Andraud*

GOOSSENS, E.	Suite	Op. 6	*Chester*
b. 1893	fl, vn, harp (or pf)		
	5 Impressions of a	" 7	"
	Holiday		
	fl, vc, pf		
	Pastoral and Harle-	Op. 39	*Curwen*
	quinade		
	fl, ob, pf		
GRABNER, H.	Quartet		*Andraud*
b. 1886	fl, ob, cl, fag		
	Kleine Serenade		*Kistner & Siegel*
	fl, fag		
GRAUPNER, C.	Suite, F ma.		*Hinrichsen*
b. 1683	fl, ob (or vn), vn		
GRETRY, A.E.M.	Concerto (O)		*Andraud*
b. 1741			
GUERRINI, G.	Notturno		*Leduc*
b. 1890	fl, vn, pf		
GUILLEMAIN, L.G.	Conversation	Op. 12	*B. & H.*
b. 1705	(Klengel)		
	fl, vn, va, clav		
HAHN, R.	Romanesque		*Heugel*
b. 1875	fl, va, pf		
HANDEL, G.F.	Works include:		
b. 1685	3 Kammertrios	" 2	*B. & H.*
	(Sieffert)		
	F. ma. C mi.		
	fl, vn, vc, clav		
	G mi.		
	2 fl, vc, clav		
	Quartet, D mi.		*Schott*
	fl, vn, vc, clav		
HASSE, J.A.	Sonata		*Nagel*
b. 1699	2 fl, fag (or vc), clav		
	Concerto		*Schott*
	fl, 2 vn, clav		
	Concerto, B mi.		*B. & H.*
	(Walther)		
HAYDN, F.J.	6 Trios (Dittrich)	" 100	*Z.*
b. 1732	fl, vn, vc		
	3 Trios		*Heugel*
	fl, vc, pf		
	London Trios		*Nagel*
	2 fl, vc		
	Quartet (Upmeyer)		"
	fl, vn, va, pf		

HAYDN, M.	Divertimento, D ma.		*Hofmeister*
b. 1737	fl, ob, horn, fag		
HEINICHEN, J.D.	Sonata	Op. 8	*B. & H.*
b. 1683	fl, ob, clav		
	Concerto, G ma.		*C.F. Vieweg*
	fl, 2 vn, clav		*(Musica Rara)*
HENNESSY, S.	Variations on a Theme	Op. 58	*Eschig*
b. 1886	of 6 Notes		
	fl, vn, va, vc		
HOFFMEISTER, F.A.	Concerto, D ma. (O)		*Sikorski*
b. 1754			
HOLBROOKE, J.	2 Suites	*Modern Music Library*	
b. 1878	fl, cl, pf		
	Quartet	,,	,, ,,
	fl, ob, cl, fag		
HÖLLER, K.	Divertimento	Op. 11	*Willy Müller*
n. 1907	fl, vn, va, vc, pf		
HOLST, G.	Terzetto		*Chester*
b. 1874	fl, ob, va		
HONEGGER, A.	Rhapsody		*Senart*
b. 1892	pf, 2 fl, cl		
	Contrepoints:		
	No. 1		*Chester*
	fl, vc		
	No. 3		*Hansen*
	fl, cor angl, vn, vc		
HUGUES, L.	Quartet		*Chester*
b. 1836	fl, ob, cl, fag		
IBERT, J.	Entracte		*Leduc*
b. 1890	fl, guitar		
	Aria		,,
	fl, vn (or cl), pf		
	2 Interludes		,,
	fl, vn, pf (or harp)		
	2 Mouvements		,,
	2 fl, cl, fag		
	Concerto (O)		,,
INDY, V.D'	Suite en parties	Op. 91	*Rouart Lerolle*
b. 1851	harp, fl, va, vc		
INGENHOVEN, J.	Trio		*Senart*
b. 1876	fl, cl, harp		
JACOB, G.	3 Inventions		*Jos. Williams*
b. 1895	fl, ob		
	Concerto (str. O)		,, ,,

JACOBSON, M.	Suite		*Augener*
b. 1896	fl, ob, pf		
JANITSCH, J.G.	Chamber Sonata	Op. 8	*B. & H.*
b. 1708	fl, ob, gamb, harp-sichord		
JEMNITZ, A.	2 Trios		*Z.*
b. 1899	fl, vn, va	" 19	
	fl, ob, cl	" 20	
JOLIVET, A.	Pastorales de Noël		*Heugel*
b. 1905	fl, fag, harp		
	Sonatine		*Boosey & Hawkes*
	fl, cl		
	Alla Rustica	"	"
	fl, harp		
KEISER, R.	3 Sonatas		*Nagel*
b. 1674	fl, vn, clav		
KETTING, P.	Sonata		*Donemus*
b. 1905	fl, ob, pf		
	Trio		"
	fl, cl, fag		
KLERK, A. DE	Sarabande and Sicili-enne		*Heuwekemeyer*
b. 1917	fl, ob		
KOECHLIN, C.	Trio		*Senart*
b. 1867	fl, cl, fag		
KRAUS, J.M.	Sonata		*Nagel*
b. 1756	fl, va		
KREBS, J.L.	Trio, D ma.		*B. & H.*
b. 1713	fl, vn, vc		
LACOMBE, P.	Passepied		*Durand*
b. 1837	fl, fag		
	Dialogue		*Heugel*
	fl, fag, pf		
	Serenade	Op. 47	*Hamelle*
	fl, ob, pf		
LAJTHA, L.	2 Trios	Opp. 22, 47	*Leduc*
b. 1892	fl, vc, harp		
	Hommages	Op. 42	*Otto Junne*
	fl, vn, cl, harp		*(Munich)*
LECLAIR, J.M.	Trio Sonata	" 2, No. 8	*Schott*
b. 1697	fl, gamb (va or vc), clav		
	Concerto C ma. (str. O)		*Ricordi*
LOEILLET, J.B.	2 Trio Sonatas, C mi.		*Lemoine*
b. 1653	D mi.		
	fl, ob, pf		

LOTTI, A.	Sonata		*Z.*
b. 1667	fl, gamb, clav		
MALIPIERO, G. F.	Sonata		*U.E.*
b. 1882	fl, ob, cl, fag		
MANICKE, D.	Concerto		*Simrock*
MANZIARLY, M. DE	Trio		*U.M.P.*
b. 1900	fl, vc, pf		
MENGELBERG, K.	Trio		*Donemus*
b. 1902	fl, ob, fag		
MARTEAU, H.	Divertimento	Op. 43, No. 1	*S.M.*
b. 1874	fl, vn		
	Partita	" 42, No. 2	"
	fl, va		
MARTIN, F.	Sonate da Chiesa		*U.E.*
b. 1890	fl, org		
MARTINŮ, B.	Madrigal Sonata		*Schott*
b. 1890	fl, vn, pf		
	Promenades		*Chester*
	fl, vn, pf		"
	Trio		
	fl, vc, pf		
MATSUDAIRA, Y.	Rhymes for Severino		*Shawnee Press*
b. 1907	Gazzeloni		
	fl, perc		
MAW, N.	Chamber Music		*Chester*
b. 1935	wind quint, pf		
MIGOT, G.	Concert		*Leduc*
b. 1891	fl, vc, harp (or pf)		
	Quartet		"
	fl, cl, vn, harp		
	Divertissements		*U.M.P.*
	Nos. 1 and 2		
	fl, harp		
	No. 5		
	fl, cl, harp		
	Livre des Danceries		*Leduc*
	fl, vn, pf		
MILHAUD, D.	Sonata		*Durand*
b. 1892	fl, ob, cl, pf		
MOLIQUE, B.	Concerto		*Andraud*
b. 1802			
MORITZ, E.	Divertimento		*Z.*
b. 1891	fl, cl, fag		

MOULE-EVANS, D. b. 1905	Suite fl, ob, pf		*Jos. Williams*
MOZART, W.A. b. 1756	4 Quartets fl, vn, va, vc		*Peters*
	C ma.	K.Anh 171	
	D ma.	K 285	
	G ma.	K 285a	
	A ma.	K 298	
	12 Duets arr. fl, fag		*Ricordi*
	Rondo from K 320 (arr. Collins) fl, ob, pf		*Bosworth*
	Andante (arr. Goehr) fl, ob, va, vc	K 616	*Schott*
MULDER, E.W. b. 1898	Fuga fl, ob, cl		*Donemus*
NAUMANN, J.G. b. 1741	Quartet fl, vn, vc, clav		*Sikorski*
NIELSEN, C. b. 1865	Concerto (O)		*Chester*
PEPUSCH, J.C. b. 1667	Sonata fl, vn, clav		*Schott*
	3 Trio Sonatas fl, ob, clav		*Musica Rara*
PERGOLESI, G.B. b. 1710	Concertos: C mi. (arr. Barbirolli) (str O)		*O.U.P.*
	G ma. (Meylan) (str O)		*Boosey & Hawkes*
PETRASSI, G. b. 1904	Concerto		*Zerboni*
PEZ, J.C. b. 1664	Trio Sonata fl, vn, clav		*Peters*
PIERNÉ, G. b. 1863	Sonata da Camera fl, vc, pf	Op. 48	*Durand*
PIJPER, W. b. 1894	Trio fl, cl, fag		*Donemus*
PISTON, W. b. 1894	3 Pieces fl, cl, fag		*Andraud*
PITFIELD, T.B. b. 1903	Trio fl, ob, pf		*Augener*

PLEYEL, I.J.	3 Sonatas	Op. 16	*Kistner & Siegel*
b. 1757	fl, vc, pf		
	3 Quartets	" 20	*Doblinger*
	fl, vn, va, vc		
POSTON, E.	Trio		*Chester*
b. 1905	fl, cl, harp		
QUANTZ, J.J.	3 Trio Sonatas:		
b. 1697	D ma.		*Kistner & Siegel*
	fl, vn, clav		
	C mi.		*Z.*
	fl, ob, clav		
	F ma.		*"*
	fl, vn, clav		
RAINIER, P.	Six Pieces for five		*Schott*
b. 1903	wind instruments		
	wind quintet		
RAMEAU, J.P.	Pièces en concerts		*Durand*
b. 1683	(Saint-Saëns)		
	fl, vc, clav		
RANDS, B.	Actions for Six		*U.E.*
b. 1935	fl, va, vc, harp, 2 perc		
RAPHAEL, G.	Sonatine	Op. 65,No. 1	*B. & H.*
b. 1903	fl, va, harp		
	Quartet	" 61	*Willy Müller*
	fl, ob, cl, fag		
RATHAUS, K.	Gavotte Classique		*Boosey & Hawkes*
b. 1905	fl, ob, fag		
RAWSTHORNE, A.	Suite		*O.U.P.*
b. 1905	fl, vla, harp		
REGER, M.	2 Serenades:		
b. 1873	fl, vn, va.		
	D ma.	Op. 77a	*Peters*
	G ma.	" 141a	*"*
REINECKE, C.H.C.	Works include:		
b. 1824	Concerto, D ma. (O)	" 283	*B. & H.*
REIZENSTEIN, F.	Trio, A ma.		*Lengnick*
b. 1911	fl, ob, pf		
	Trio		*Galliard*
	fl, cl, fag		
RICHTER, F.	6 Sonatas		*Bärenreiter*
b. 1709	fl, vc, clav		
RIEGGER, W.	3 Canons		*New Music*
b. 1885	fl, ob, cl, fag		*(N.Y.)*
RIETI, V.	Sonata		*U.E.*
b. 1898	pf, fl, ob, fag		

RIISAGER, K.	Serenade		*Hansen*
b. 1897	fl, vn, vc		
	Sonata		"
	fl, cl, vn, vc		
RIVIER, J.	Concerto		*Pierre Noel*
b. 1896			
ROHOZINSKI, L.	4 Pieces		*Senart*
19th cent.	fl, vn		
RÖNTGEN, J.	Trio	Op. 86	*B. & H.*
b. 1855	fl, ob fag		
ROSENBERG, H.	Trio		*Nordiska*
b. 1892	fl, vn, va		
ROSSINI, G. A.	6 Quartets (Zachert)		*Schott*
b. 1792	fl, cl, horn, fag		
ROUSSEL, A.C.P.	Trio	" 40	*Durand*
b. 1869	fl, va, vc		
SAINT-SAËNS, C.	Caprice	" 79	"
b. 1835	pf, fl, ob, cl		
	Tarantella (O)	" 6	"
	fl, cl, pf		
SAMMARTINI, G.B.	Notturno		*B. & H.*
b. 1698	fl, 2 vn, vc		
SCARLATTI, A	Quartet		*Peters*
b. 1659	fl, 2 vn, clav		
SCHMITT, FLORENT	Sonatine	" 85	*Durand*
b. 1870	fl, cl, pf		
	Quartet		"
	fl, vn, vc, pf		
SCHUBERT, F.[1]	Quartet		*Peters*
b. 1797	fl, guitar, va, vc		
SCHULHOFF, E.	Concertino		*U.E.*
b. 1894	fl, va, db		
SCHULLER, G.	Wind Quintet		*Schott*
b. 1925			
SEIBER, M.	Pastorale		"
b. 1905	fl, vn, va, vc		
	Permutazioni a Cinque		"
	wind quintet		
SIEGL, O.	Trifolium	" 145	*Doblinger*
b. 1896	fl, ob, va		
SMIT, L.	Trio		*Senart*
b. 1900	fl, va, harp		

[1]Originally a Notturno by Matiegkas (Op. 21) for which Schubert wrote the cello part.

STAMITZ, C.	Trio	Op. 14, No. 1	*Nagel*
b. 1745	fl, vn, clav		
	2 Quartets, D ma. A ma.		*Hinrichsen*
	fl, vn, va, vc		
	Sonata	Op. 14, No. 5	*B. & H.*
	fl, vn, vc, clav		
STÖLZEL, G.	Sonata		*B. & H.*
b. 1690	fl, vn, clav		
SUK, J.	Bagatelle	*Hudebni Matice (Artia)*	
b. 1874	fl, vn, pf		
SZALOWSKI, A.	Duo	*Omega (Chester)*	
b. 1907	fl, cl		
SZERVANSKY, E.	Trio		*Kultura*
b. 1912	fl, vn, va		
TARTINI, G.	Concerto (str. O)		*Sikorski*
b. 1692			
TELEMANN, G.P.	Works include:		
b. 1681	6 Suites		*Bärenreiter*
	fl, vn, clav		
	Duet, G ma.		*Nagel*
	fl, vn		
	Trios:		
	F ma. fl, va, clav		,,
	E ma. fl, vn, clav		,,
	E mi, fl, ob, clav		*Bärenreiter*
	Quartets:		
	D mi. 2 fl, recorder, clav		*B. & H.*
	F ma. fl, ob, vn, clav		*Schott*
	D ma. fl, vn, vc, clav		*Z.*
	G mi. fl, vn, gamb, clav		,,
	B mi. fl, vn, vc, clav		*Nagel*
	E mi. fl, vn, vc, clav		,,
	G ma. fl, ob, vn, clav		*Peters*
	Concertos:		
	G ma. fl, 2 vn, clav		*Bärenreiter*
	G mi. fl, 2 vn, clav		*Schott*
THOMSON, V.	Concerto		*Ricordi*
b. 1896			
TOCCHI, G.	Notturno, Canzona and		*Santis*
b. 1901	Ballo		
	fl, va, harp		

TOMASI, H. b. 1901	Pastorale Inca fl, 2 vn		*Leduc*
	Concerto, F ma. (O)		*"*
TURCHI, G. b. 1916	Trio fl, cl, va		*Schott*
VILLA-LOBOS, H. b. 1887	Choros, No. 2 fl, cl		*Eschig*
	Bachianas Brasileiras, No. 6 fl, fag		*Schott*
	Quartet fl, ob, cl, fag		*"*
VIVALDI, A. b. 1680	Sonata, A mi. (Malipiero) fl, fag, clav		*Ricordi*
	Pastorale (Upmeyer) fl, vc, clav		*Nagel*
	Concertos: G mi. fl, ob, fag D ma. fl, vn, fag (or vc) G mi. fl, vn, fag, clav A mi. fl, 2 vn, clav F ma. fl, vn, fag, clav D ma. fl, vn, fag, clav		*Ricordi*
WAILLY, P. DE b. 1854	Aubade fl, ob, cl		*Rouart*
	Sérénade fl, vn, ca, vc		*"*
WEBER, C.M. VON b. 1786	Trio pf, fl, vc	Op. 63	*Peters*
WECKERLIN, J.B. b. 1821	Pastorale fl, ob, pf		*Heugel*
WEIS, F. b. 1898	Trio fl, cl, fag		*Samfundet (Chester)*
WEISSMANN, J. b. 1879	Kammermusik fl, va, pf	" 86	*Willy Müller*
WIDOR, C.M. b. 1845	Serénade fl, vn, pf	" 10	*Hamelle*
WIENER, K. b. 1891	3 Pieces fl, cor angl, cl	" 20	*U.E.*
WOOD, Hugh b. 1932	Trio fl, va, pf		*"*

ZACHAU, F.W.	Trio	*Kistner & Siegel*
b. 1663	fl, fag, clav	
ZAGWIJN, H.	Introduction and	*Donemus*
b. 1878	Scherzo	
	fl, va, harp	
	Pastorale and Scherzo	,,
	fl, ob, pf	
	Sonata	,,
	fl, cl pf	
	2 Trios	,,
	fl, ob, cl.	